1250

CONVERSION TO JUDAISM

CONVERSION TO JUDAISM:
From the Biblical Period to the Present

Joseph R. Rosenbloom

Hebrew Union College Press
Cincinnati, Ohio 1978

Library of Congress Cataloging in Publication Data

Rosenbloom, Joseph R
  Conversion to Judaism.

  Bibliography: p.
  Includes index.
  1. Proselytes and proselyting, Jewish. I. Title.
BM729.P7R67   296.7'1   78-9409
ISBN 0-87820-113-0

MANUFACTURED IN THE UNITED STATES OF AMERICA

This book is published under the auspices of the Rabbinic Alumni Association of Hebrew Union College-Jewish Institute of Religion. A quinquennial fund to which its members contribute is set aside for the specific purpose of encouraging members of the Association to pursue studies in Judaism with the prospect of publication.

JORDAN PEARLSON
President, Rabbinic Alumni
Association

WALTER JACOB
Chairman, Publications Committee
of the Rabbinic Alumni
Association

For Deborah, Eve, and Dena

Table of Contents

Part V: After the French Revolution

Introduction

IN BIBLICAL times the Hebrews, like all other peoples, had to develop a way of viewing their group identity that would both encourage group cohesion and allow outsiders to join the tribe as equals. The problem of how to keep Jewish identity meaningful and at the same time make entrance into Judaism possible has continued throughout Jewish history, and not surprisingly is still central in the United States of the 1970s. In some periods exclusivistic views prevailed and conversion was discouraged. At other times—during the Roman Empire, for example—conversion or partial conversion was so easy that Judaism's distinctive quality was in danger of being dissolved beyond recognition.

In the Hebrew-Jewish experience, a unique invention made it possible to extend the bonds of membership beyond the traditional blood ties of tribal society. Through the primal father, Abraham, the tribe was bound in a covenant to a supernatural father, Yahweh, or God. The ramifications of this relationship to God were manifold. New members were able to come into the tribe, or a group of related tribes, through adherence to the Yahweh-covenant. In this way the tribe's growth possibilities were dramatically extended beyond what was possible through biological reproduction. A religious system was developed to give content to the covenant with the deity. It served to tie the faithful to one another as well as to the deity. On occasion the interests of the religious system became more important than those of the social organization, but religion did prove effective in binding large groups together.

While religion served to bring disparate groups together, outsiders were still treated with suspicion and exclusion. Throughout Jewish history, in spite of the theoretical welcome to the covenant, restrictions and difficulties were present. It is the thesis of this study that in most instances the actual practice and attitude of Jews toward persons joining them was determined by the concrete situation at the time. Openness to new affiliates, or converts, is Judaism's general tendency, but a sufficient number of tribal elements remained, and still remain, to cause the occasional erection of barriers. These attitudes developed slowly and continued long after their original purpose was forgotten, even when they became counterproductive and seriously harmful. Similarly, gentiles joined themselves to Judaism, whether as individuals or in groups, only when it served their interests to do so. The same motivation of personal advantage lay behind Judaism's welcome to converts and occasional hostility to them.

This volume includes a review of the literature concerned with conversion to Judaism and an interpretation of the course of conversion through Jewish history. It begins with the biblical period, continues with the Middle Ages, when religious conversion began to lose much of its appeal in Europe, and ends with an account of the contemporary situation, including the general decline of institutional religion as the primary social organization in the West.

The development of popular and institutional ideologies is an ancillary interest of this study. Most Jews and gentiles nowadays believe that Judaism is, and generally has been, hostile to proselyting. This attitude is reflected in the lack of virtually any Jewish proselyting in contemporary society. It is usually defended by erroneous interpretations of the prohibitions of intermarriage by Ezra and Nehemiah, the oft-quoted talmudic statement that a convert is like an "itching boil" on Judaism, and the Christian and Muslim prohibitions of Jewish proselyting. Actually, proselyting was once widespread among Jews but fell into disuse because of concrete environmental factors. Despite overwhelming evidence to the contrary, great credence has been given to the theory that Jews never actively sought converts. The change in attitude and the acceptance of this ideology took centuries. It should not be surprising, therefore, if it takes a considerable period to restore the original attitude, now that conditions make Jewish proselyting possible again and necessary.

The Jewish people in recent decades have suffered the loss of six million members in World War II and are threatened with the loss of millions of others through cultural genocide in Russia and elsewhere in

Eastern Europe. Coupled with this is the gradually increasing rate of mixed marriage between Jews and gentiles, and the general loss to Judaism of the children of such marriages. Finally, ever-larger numbers of Jews are becoming emotionally and intellectually alienated from Judaism. A return to active proselyting by the organized Jewish community might compensate for the losses resulting from these three phenomena.

PART I
THE BIBLICAL PERIOD

1

The Conquest and Settlement of the Land

THE INVASION of territory is always accompanied by some kind of accommodation with the indigenous population. The conquered people may be either destroyed totally, driven from their land, maintained amidst the conquerors as subservients, or assimilated by those who have overwhelmed them. There is considerable controversy concerning the Israelite conquest and settlement of the land of Canaan as well as the destiny of the conquered peoples following the invasion. Because the evidence, both literary and archaeological, is open to more than one interpretation, no single explanation has been universally accepted. Several of them are, indeed, contradictory.

Martin Noth, the leading disciple of the Alt school of biblical interpretation, accepts little of the biblical narrative as historical. This is particularly so of the account of the conquest of Canaan outlined in the Book of Joshua. In Noth's interpretation, Israel appears as the father of the twelve ancestors and heroes (*eponymi*) for whom the tribes of Israel were named (Gen. 32:29). The name *Israel* was used for a person or as a collective term, he maintains, and there is no trace of evidence concerning how the group of twelve tribes acquired it and whether it had a previous history.[1] Further, the tribes never acted as a unit—certainly not for any substantial period. A temporary union existed during the time of Saul, but prior to that time they operated as individual tribes or, occasionally, as small groups of tribes which were united geographically, linguistically, and religiously but not as a nation.

The Israelite settlement of Canaan, according to Noth, began about 1200 B.C.E., when the invaders entered those parts of the country which were only sparsely settled or had not been settled at all.[2] These were

3

chiefly high places since the plains were held by the older Canaanite population, which was concentrated in cities, and alongside which the invading tribes now lived as a new element. Unlike the account given in the Book of Joshua, military battles were few and of minor importance. The early settlement was fairly quiet and peaceful, following the general pattern observed when semi-nomadic breeders of small cattle from adjoining steppes and deserts pass into settled life. This process took several centuries.[3] The exodus is also seen as gradual, with the elements involved in it gaining a tribal identity only when finally in Canaan. While they may have had some tribal identity in Egypt, it is difficult to determine precisely what it was.

Because Israel had an advanced system of unification and occasional power, conquered neighbors were assimilated into the Israelite system. This took place gradually because the Jewish system itself was not fully developed when the Israelites arrived in Canaan. The very fact that the Israelites believed their system superior led them to absorb conquered peoples whenever possible rather than follow any one of the other methods of dealing with them. This was particularly true during periods of great expansion, such as those during the reigns of David and Jeroboam. The formation of the Jewish nation was the result of the historical situation in Canaan. The Israelite tribes were more powerful than their neighbors, but at the same time, the emerging Israelite nation threatened the integrity of the individual tribes.[4]

A disciple of the Alt-Noth school, Norman Gottwald, favors the idea of "settlement" of Canaan rather than the biblical account of a "national conquest" because it more clearly allows for the resultant merging of the Canaanites into the Israelite nation during and subsequent to the reign of David. The Gibeonites, who tricked the Israelite conquerors into an alliance and then became a servant-people, are seen as the prototype of the indigenous peoples who joined themselves to the invaders. Realizing their weakness, the Gibeonites sought to avoid annihilation or expulsion by joining the conquerors on conditions as favorable as possible (Josh. 9). While they initially were servants, they presumably eventually became assimilated into the Jewish nation.

According to Gottwald, other reasons for viewing the conquest as gradual are found in the biblical narrative itself.

1. The indigenous nations were not destroyed in a single sweep, in order to prevent the land from becoming a desolate, uninhabited

wilderness (Deut. 7:22). A rapid complete conquest would make the incorporation of the conquered impossible.

2. Some of the Canaanite nations were left to test Israel's loyalty to God, otherwise their pride might lead them to abandon their faith (Judg. 2:21).

3. They were also left to teach future generations the arts of war (Judg. 3:2).

4. A number of areas were specifically noted as remaining to be conquered, among them the coastal plain from Egypt to Sidon, the walled cities, excepting Hazor, and Jerusalem (Josh. 11:13, 13:2–6, 15:63).

The settlement of Canaan is therefore viewed, as noted by Noth, as taking place over a period of centuries prior to, concurrent with, and subsequent to the Egyptian sojourn and the exodus. Joshua's dramatic attack was but one important phase of the occupation, but the process of settlement began with the patriarchs and continued until the time of David. Moses and Joshua, members of the northern tribes, encouraged the latent unity of the tribes and were the first to elicit the veneration of all or most of them. Later, veneration was extended to the heroes of the other groups that were eventually consolidated. These included Abraham, Isaac, and Jacob.

Gottwald structures the Israelites into northern and southern units. The northern, or Jacob, tribes had centers in Bethel and Shechem. They came from Mesopotamia and were probably of Aramean origin. A splinter group broke away and went to Egypt, probably for economic reasons, but it maintained a memory of its affinity with the Jacob tribes which remained in Canaan. Moses was the leader of the Egyptian clans at the time of the liberation. Through his contact with his father-in-law, a Midianite priest named Jethro, he learned of the southern Hebrews and of Yahweh. It was probably Moses who unified these two groups. The southern, or Abraham, tribes entered Canaan from the south and had their center at Hebron. This group was composed of elements which had migrated from Mesopotamia and of "Judean" elements which were partly of Midianite-Kenite origin. The Judean peoples were probably from the desert regions of Arabia and joined with the Abraham element in the Negev, absorbing native Canaanites at the same time. The result, an amalgam of migratory Amorite and Arabian groups on Canaanite soil, is seen as the source of the tribe of Judah.

Since the union of Jacob and Abraham "groups" was only one of many contenders for the control of Canaan, why was it successful? In addition to nomadic elan, which the others had also, it had the Mosaic Yahwism, which produced a remarkable unity in spite of strong counter-currents of division and fragmentation. Later, in the eleventh century B.C.E., when the Canaanites and Israelites were united against the Philistines, an Aegean people, a way was needed to assimilate the Canaanites if Israel was to be the successor people. With Albright, Gottwald sees in the religion of Moses a missionary faith with the dynamic appeal necessary to accomplish this end.[5]

Johannes Pedersen falls within the general orientation of the Alt-Noth school. He maintains that the tribes of Israel formed only during the settlement period in Canaan. Abraham immigrated from the east and settled in Hebron. Jacob was connected partly with the founder of the Edomites, partly with the Arameans, and finally with the Israelite tribes that lived in Egypt and Sinai, and later migrated to Canaan. The narratives of the moving and settling, developed long after the events, are permeated with the spirit of later Israel but based on old traditions. Much of the early history is impenetrable, but some suppositions may be made.

Thus, the tribe of Reuben, the firstborn of Jacob, while quite insignificant and living east of the Jordan in historical times, was once settled west of the Jordan and must have been an important tribe. Among the many other questions which may be raised from the biblical account, one pertains to Zebulon and Reuben, who had the same mother but had nothing to do with one another in historical times. The later contrivance of these tribes being descended from Jacob met the need of explaining the conquest and assimilation of Canaanite peoples. According to Pedersen's interpretation, Jacob seems to have been a tribal or local name which was taken over by the Israelites. It probably resulted from the coalescing of two tribes, becoming the nucleus around which the Israelites formed.[6] Somewhat similarly, the Joseph tribe disappeared and was merged into the tribal formations of Ephraim and Manasseh, who, according to the biblical narrative, are the sons of Joseph.[7] Pedersen discerns no antagonism between the Israelites and the Canaanites—the latter merged ino the Israelite unity and disappeared, but in the process infused Canaanite life and culture into Israel.

The system of twelve Hebrew tribes became formalized as a result of the Priestly writer's interpretation and rewriting of Jewish history. This history, written in the exilic and post-exilic periods (after the destruction of Jerusalem and the exile of much of the Judean population to Babylonia in 586 B.C.E.), includes both books of Chronicles as well as sections of the Pentateuch and the historical books. Scholars see it as generally artificial, made to conform to the interests of the Priestly school and its understanding of the needs of the Jewish people. Indicative of the artificiality of this system is its viewing of the few hundred freebooters who rallied around David as regular clans (1 Sam. 22:1 f.; 1 Chron. 12). It was not difficult to systematize the tribal structure since at the time of the Priestly writer the tribes were of no practical importance.

The tribal names may only have indicated territories. In a later period, the tribes were not what they had been earlier, extended families. As Israel developed, conquered more territory, and moved into cities, the tribes were of little importance, but because of tradition, they still kept a place in the literature. The Canaanites, as a conquered people, became lamas or corvée-workers (Josh. 16:10, 17:13; Judg. 1:28, 30, 33, 35; 1 Kings 9:21). While some Israelites also functioned in this role, "the Canaanites were corvée-workers par excellence and were therefore designated as citizens of lower rank." [8] Pedersen sees these reduced Canaanites as *gerim*, or sojourners. *Ger* (*gerim*, plural) is therefore the term used to designate anyone living in association with a community which originally was not his own. He may even be an Israelite (Judg. 17:7–9, 19:16). It is a general term which did not include all foreigners but only those who formed a limited social class of conquered and otherwise subjugated peoples. They then became closely but never wholly assimilated. [9] The various categories of the Israelite population and their role in society will be discussed further.

John Bright's major criticism of the Alt-Noth school centers on its general disparagement of the historicity of the biblical text, ignoring what he considers the profound results of archaeology. A disciple of Albright, Bright generally accepts the conquest of Canaan as outlined in the Book of Joshua, noting that it led to large numbers of people, including whole clans and cities, coming into the Israelite ranks en masse. At the same time, he agrees with those who view the tribal system as a developing one which was in flux over a long period. In substantiating his position, he makes the following points:

1. Among the clans of Manasseh (Josh. 17:2 f.) are Hepher, Tirsah, and Shechem. The first two are listed as Canaanite cities conquered

by Israel (Josh. 12:17, 24), with Shechem also a Canaanite (Amorite) city which still had a non-Israelite population in the period of the Judges, with a temple to Baalberith, god of the covenant, a local deity (Judg. 9). Gradually they were absorbed in the tribal structure of Manasseh.

2. The listing of Reuben, Simeon, and Levi as the eldest of the twelve sons of Jacob implies that they were once mighty tribes, probably living in Canaan before the conquest took place. Following the conquest they were reduced in strength. Reuben, exposed to Moabite depredations, virtually vanished by the eleventh century. Simeon lost its independence early and was absorbed into Judah (Josh. 19:1–9). Levi ceased being a secular tribe although there is evidence that it was once warlike (Gen. 34 and 49:5–7). Its name was applied to those having priestly duties.

Bright also feels that it is impossible to say which tribes left Egypt in the exodus. The group led by Moses was a mixed rabble, but at Sinai, where "it received its peculiar faith and was organized in covenant as the people of Yahweh," it became the nucleus of Israel.[10] It had no tribal structure in Egypt; rather, it was comprised of slaves of various tribal backgrounds, and they picked up others during the sojourn in the wilderness who were converted to the new faith. These, together with whole clans, later filled out Israel's tribal system. Juggling of the tribal system and the importance of the number twelve is seen in the following:

1. The loss of Levi as a secular tribe is filled by Ephraim and Manasseh.
2. Manasseh or a part of it was at one time known as Machir (Judg. 5:14, Josh. 17:1).
3. The population of the Gilead highlands was mixed, made up of Gadite and Josephite elements (Num. 32:39 f., Josh. 13:24–31), and was designated as Gilead (Judg. 5:17, 11:1 f.).
4. Once the system was stabilized, it did not change (Gen. 49, Deut. 33), even after the troubles of Reuben and Simeon. Manasseh continued as one tribe even after it split into eastern and western sections.[11]

As far as Bright is concerned, what made Israel unique, different from her neighbors, was not language, habitat, or national culture, but faith. "Israel was a people precisely because of her faith. The history of Israel, therefore, is not the history of a Twelve-Clan League, nor of a nation; it is the history of a faith and its people."[12] Thus, while a great deal of the conquest and settlement of Canaan may be recaptured from both literary remains and archaeology, the most crucial item in the understanding of the whole process is the religion of Israel.

Almost the opposite of these descriptions of the conquest and settlement of Canaan is the reconstruction proposed by Yehezkel Kaufmann. He maintains that there was a "unified conquest of Canaan by a confederation of tribes that fought to carry out a preconceived national plan of conquest." [13] If they had not been united at the beginning of the conquest, the subsequent events and circumstances in Canaan would have rent them apart. (Of course, this is just what happened.) He also argues that there was no culture-contact with the Canaanites and that the Canaanites did not influence the Israelites in any way. In all the early biblical accounts, he says, the Israelites are depicted as hostile toward the Canaanites. It is only in later documents that the Israelites are shown to have been unsuccessful in driving the Canaanites out, thus making alliances with them, intermarrying, and committing idolatry.

That scholars hold otherwise, Kaufmann writes, is the result of their confusing the maps of Israel detailed in the Bible. First, there is the "ideal" or utopian map, which included Philistia, Tyre, Sidon, Lebanon, and from the Jordan River on the east to the sea on the west, from the Sea of Suf in the south to the Euphrates in the north. This map, including some twenty nations (which might lead to the conclusion that there was a mixed population in Israel), does not reflect any historical situation. It is a very ancient map produced before both the conquest of Canaan and the establishment of the kingdom. Excluding the Transjordan, its size does not correspond to the early and late kingdoms.

Four other maps are found in the biblical text by Kaufmann, each corresponding to historical changes.

1. Moses' Land of Israel: This map reflects the discrepancy between the ancient promise (in the first map) and the actual situation. It does, however, include Transjordan (Num. 21:21–35).
2. Joshua's Land of Israel: This map includes Transjordan but not the northern territory of Dan. It comprises three parts, one conquered but not allotted, one allotted but not conquered, and one neither allotted nor conquered. This was a dynamic period when boundaries were considered temporary (Josh. 1–Judg. 3).
3. The Real Land of Israel: This map took shape as a result of the wars during the period of the Judges. It encompasses the area of

ethnic Israel, the land where only Israelites were to live. It was to be their home but they were not to rule over others. Non-Israelites in this area were extirpated or expelled. The map was based on the promise to the Israelites from the time of the patriarchs.

4. Israelite Empire: This contains the ethnic land of Israel, but as the result of imperialism, it also includes the coast, Edom, Moab, Ammon, and Aram.

Following the biblical statements regarding the Canaanites, Kaufmann says that the Canaanite population and cultural factors were eliminated in the "real land of Israel" as early as the beginning of the period of the Judges. Contrary to most other opinions, he states that at no stage was the conquest of the land of Canaan a process of peaceful settlement. It did not produce national and cultural intermingling. The Canaanite element was defeated and driven out. He further sees Canaan as having been composed of a hodgepodge of peoples, and these, he says, were defeated by Israelite unity, which had been forged through a religio-national covenant made by the tribes in the wilderness. Kaufmann comes to this conclusion through the biblical accounts of the conquest as well as the absence, in his opinion, of any general ethnic and cultural amalgam of peoples in Israelite Palestine. Though there was no mass assimilation of Canaanites in Israel, ethnic units such as Calebites, Jerahmeelites, and Rechabites were assimilated culturally, although they each maintained their own ethnic individuality. Even the Calebites, he argues, who lived with the Israelites and were culturally absorbed by them, did not lose their ethnic identity or name. They remained a separate and inferior caste even after they became "God-fearing" Jews. In any event, these and other similar peoples, including *gerim*, were not Canaanites. Any Canaanite influence, Kaufmann insists, took place outside the "real land" of Israel.

The *herem*, or exclusion, of the Canaanites kept them apart and prevented their absorption into the class of *gerim* or even slaves, let alone the class of free men of Israel. While the *herem* may be seen as terrible, it had important social and religious consequences. Israel did not assimilate into the indigenous population. Materially this brought a marked decline, but it also provided Israel's religion with an environment in which it could grow, free of the influences of the popular pagan cult.[14]

As divergent as are some of the interpretations of the conquest and settlement, those of Kaufmann and of the Uppsala school of Sweden are so different that one may be led to wonder whether they are referring to the same people and events. In contradistinction to Kaufmann, Engnell, a leading spokesman for the Uppsala school, writes: "The victory of the Canaanite cult is practically complete. To look for the peculiarly 'Israelite' or 'nomadic' element is extremely difficult, not to say hopeless. . . . And the fact that the Canaanite cult is victorious means in reality that the Canaanite religion is victorious. . . . Nevertheless, as already indicated, it is unmistakable that a new stamp, a new touch, is given by the desert blood to the development in its entirety." [15]

Further, this school views God, whom Moses knew as Yahweh, as the old West Semitic high god variously known as El, El elyon, Shalem, and Sedek, and worshipped as El by the patriarchs. He was activated by Moses and so became the God of the Israelites. Because the El who was worshipped in Canaan was originally identical with the God of Moses, it was easier for the fusion to take place. For the Hebrews, the conquest of Canaan led not to retrogression but to an advance. Other contributions from the Canaanites included the idea of messianism and the belief in resurrection. Further, the Uppsala school has concluded that the substance of the Pentateuch, except for much of the legal material, was transmitted orally until the exilic and post-exilic period, when it was gradually fixed in writing. Because of this it is virtually impossible to isolate the various documentary components which may comprise the oral tradition. If this view is correct, then it is impossible to range the material chronologically, and even more difficult to reconstruct the early history of Israel. All the history that is known is what the final, fixed form tells us, and there is no foundation for having a real history of Israel. [16]

While differing with the Uppsala school in many respects, Harry Orlinsky also believes that it is not yet possible to write a thoroughly acceptable history of Israel, conforming to the highest standards of modern scientific historiography. Moreover, in spite of the results of modern archaeology and biblical studies, such a history may never be possible. Two reasons for this pessimism are given. First, "the sources are inadequate and of uncertain authorship and date." [17] Even "when two schools agree, there is no assurance that their common viewpoint is correct." [18] Second, it is extremely difficult to determine "the fundamental economic, social and political forces from documents couched almost exclusively in religious terminology and given to interpreting all human experience as manifestations of divine intervention." [19]

While G. E. Mendenhall believes that there is a respectable consensus that Israel "grew suddenly from a small religious group of clansmen to a large organization" because "the religious community of Israel was much preferable to the social and political system under which [the Canaanites and their clients] had lived previously," [20] the fact remains that the reservations of many scholars, particularly Orlinsky, must be seriously considered. Only a portion of the available interpretations have been outlined. Each of them deals with the self-same problem which has defied resolution.

Another approach is, therefore, suggested. Rather than attempt to resolve the problem of the settlement in its initial stages, we might better examine the more established and organized periods of Israelite history in order to determine the kind of environment the Israelites came into and what they did to it. As in the remainder of this study, the controlling principle will be the method of becoming a part of Israelite society and the attitude of Israelite society toward those who joined themselves to it. Every society has the task of organizing itself. The more sophisticated formalize this process by establishing legal codes. This was done by ancient Israelite society, which had the task of structuring not only its own people but the many who joined with them voluntarily as well as those whom they conquered.

2

The Inhabitants of the Land of Israel

REGARDLESS of the interpretation of the conquest and settlement of the land of Israel that one favors, the biblical narrative makes it clear that the invaders were as highly diverse as the peoples among whom they settled in Canaan. Abraham and his family came from far-off Ur and added to their family composition in Haran. The early sojourn in Canaan by the patriarchs must have added further local peoples, as did the long stay in Egypt. More important, from the point of view of outside influence, was the mixed Egyptian multitude which joined the Israelites in the exodus. To these must be added the elements which attached themselves during the period of wandering. Once the Israelites and their associates entered Canaan and began the conquest and settlement, both in Canaan and in contiguous territories, many other peoples appear to have joined, both voluntarily and out of necessity. Even if there was no mixing with Canaanites, as Kaufmann insists, there were more than twenty other peoples in close proximity (Gen. 10:15–18, 14:7, 15:19–21; Num. 13:22; Deut. 2:23; Josh. 13:2 f.). In addition, there was a constant flow of peoples throughout the fertile crescent. Thus, one of the crucial problems for the Israelites was to bring all these peoples together as a social-political unit. In order to accomplish this, it was necessary to devise a process of conversion to the Israelite national-religious system. Begun during the biblical period, this process of conversion continued throughout Jewish history. It developed and changed even as the historical situation of the Jews and Judaism changed.

Rostovtzeff was correct when he wrote that we have "not even an approximate idea of the density of the population" of Jews in the Hellenistic world.[1] Moreover, the range of estimates—from Josephus'

13

10,000,000–12,000,000 to Juster's 5,000,000, Baron's 1,100,000, Beloch's 1,000,000, and Harnack's 500,000—would lead one to despair of any sensible estimate. C. C. McCown's study of population in Palestine is based on considerations from antiquity as well as modern studies of the land.[2] Considering the size of the land and the possible population per square mile, no ancient data available even approximate an accurate estimate. McCown's studies lead him to estimate the population in 66 C.E. at 100,000 in the Galilee, 100,000 in Judah outside of Jerusalem, and 100,000 in Jerusalem. Including the population in other areas of Palestine, the total would remain under 500,000.[3] De Vaux, basing himself on the biblical text, comes up with a considerably higher figure for the period of the kings.[4] Clearly the number indicated for the exodus—600,000 foot-soldiers, their families, and the mixed multitude, all together totaling well over 3,000,000—is out of the question (Exod. 12:37–38). Equally exaggerated is the figure of 603,550 men over twenty plus 22,000 Levites older than one month and 8,580 between thirty and fifty (Num. 26:5–51, 62). The census taken in the time of David counts 800,000 men liable for military service in Israel with another 500,000 in Judah (2 Sam. 24:1–9; the parallel passage in 1 Chron. 21:1–6 has a higher figure for Israel). A sounder estimate is available from the reign of Menahem when, in 738, Tiglath-Pileser imposed a tribute of 1,000 talents of silver. To pay it Menahem levied a tax on all of the *chail gibborim* (mighty men of wealth) of 50 shekels each (2 Kings 15:19 f.). With 3,000 shekels to the talent, there would be 60,000 heads of households who enjoyed a certain prosperity. With their wives and children, this would give a total of perhaps 300,000–400,000. By adding the lower classes, artisans, poor, foreigners, and slaves, the total might reach 800,000. Whether this figure is accepted or one of the others, either lower or higher, only a percentage could have arrived in the exodus, and many of those were themselves non-Israelites. The number of people, therefore, who had to be integrated into Israelite society was the major part of the whole.

Added to these throughout the period of the kingdoms and after the exile were a great number of intermarriages. Judah and Simeon took Canaanite wives. Joseph married an Egyptian, who gave birth to Ephraim and Manasseh. Abraham came from Aram, where he and his descendants took wives for their sons. Thus, Israel is depicted as an ethnic mixture. Later Samson married a Philistine, David a Geshurite,

Solomon wives from Egypt, Moab, Ammon, Edom, and Sidon. The large number of intermarriages within the community at the time of Ezra and Nehemiah was seen as a threat not because they were inter-marriages per se, but because the wives had not been integrated into the Jewish system. The tension between desiring the integration of gentiles through conversion and maintaining aloofness from others has remained a part of the Jewish ethos since antiquity.

The classic instance of a people joining themselves to the Israelites is that of the Gibeonites (Josh. 9). Through stealth, according to the biblical account, the Gibeonites were spared the fate of the other peoples the Israelites confronted in Canaan. In any event, in later times they were still present as an identifiable group within the Jewish system as servants of the Temple. Together with such other groups as the Calebites, Jerahmeelites, Rechabites, Kenites, and Kenizzites, the Gibeonites were integrated into Israelite society, assimilating the culture while remaining socially distinct.

3
Categories of
Inhabitants of Israel

WHILE there is little likelihood that the period of the conquest and settlement of Canaan can ever be reconstructed with any accuracy, it is clear that there was a great intermingling of the Israelites with the peoples living in the territory they conquered and those constantly traversing the new nation. The flow of peoples from one place to another was constant in the Middle East. They migrated because their home conditions became intolerable: famine or other natural disasters forced them out; reports of great opportunities led many to try another locale; mercenaries were required by a newly emerging dynasty promising outstanding rewards; semi-nomadic peoples took the occasion of the establishment of a new state to settle down. Evidence of each of these kinds of movements into the new nation of Israel is apparent in the Bible. This was shown in the preceding chapters and will now be further verified by descriptions of the various classes of inhabitants in Israel. Once again, while it is impossible to be absolutely certain of the date of given developments or to accurately describe a given class, it is obvious that these classes existed and were taken into account when the legal codes were structured. The various codes span many centuries and are intermingled in the biblical text.

In order to delineate the limits of citizenship in the Israelite community, and before considering the gradations within these limits, the status situation of the full Israelite citizen and of the complete alien should be described. The term *ezrach* is exclusively utilized in the Bible to denote the homeborn Israelite—the indigenous native Israelite. "You shall have one statute, both for the stranger, and for him that is born in the land [*ezrach*]" (Num. 9:14; cf. Exod. 12:38, Num. 15:13, Ezek.

16

47:22). This was understood by the translators of the Septuagint when they rendered *ezrachi* (Pss. 88:1, 89:1) as Ισραηλίτη (Israelite). The same word is used to denote an indigenous tree (Ps. 37:35).

Contrasted with the *ezrach*, the native Israelite, is the foreigner or alien. Here, two terms are used in the Bible: *zar* and *nachri*. The first is more general and may not have been a legal term, but the second does seem to have a place in the legal codes. *Zar*, usually translated as "stranger," actually denotes foreignness with the added quality of inferiority of status. In a more general sense, it seems to indicate an individual who, for some reason, is different from the usual. An Israelite may be called a *zar* (Hos. 5:7). So may a prostitute mentioned in relationship to a non-prostitute (Prov. 2:16). Often non-Israelites are so designated (Exod. 29:33, 30:33; Isa. 1:7). In one passage *zar* simply means anyone, Israelite or not, other than the two women who came before Solomon each protesting that the child was hers (1 Kings 3:18). While *zar* and *nachri* are often used synonymously, *zar* has no specialized meaning, denotes no particular class within biblical society, and is to be seen as a general term which may be used to characterize anything outside the norm (cf. Exod. 30:9, Num. 3:4, Prov. 5:3, 7:5, 11:15, 14:10, 23:33).

The *nachri* is more clearly and particularly a stranger or foreigner who is a member of a class alien to Israelite society. "Then said the king [David] to Ittai the Gittite: 'Wherefore goest thou also with us? Return, and abide with the king; for thou art a *foreigner*, and also an exile; return to thine own place'" (2 Sam. 15:19). The holder of this special status has fewer rights. For instance, to prevent a foreigner from ruling over an Israelite, a *nachri* may not become king over Israel (Deut. 17:15).

Just who the *nachri* is, is made absolutely clear: "Moreover concerning the *nachri* that is not of thy people Israel" (1 Kings 8:41; cf. Ezra 10:2). Further, interest could be exacted of the *nachri* but not of a fellow Israelite (Deut. 23:20). While debts owed by Israelites were cancelled in the seventh, or *shemitta*, year, debts owed by a *nachri* were maintained (Deut. 15:3).

A *nachri* who indicated that he wanted to join the Israelites was granted a different status and given a different label, that of *ger*. The latter, having indicated his intention to join the people of Israel, would be brought to God's holy mountain and his sacrifices would be accepted

(Isa. 56:3, 6 f.). On the other hand, those who remained outside the "holy" community were to be cleared out (Neh. 13:30).

The differences between the *nachri* and the Israelite were not racial, since foreigners were accepted into the holy community. For this to take place a new allegiance had to be formalized. The Israelites saw themselves as a holy people (Deut. 7:6) whose land was not to be defiled (Deut. 21:33) but to be cleansed of foreign elements (Neh. 13:30). The instruction to kill and cast out the peoples of Canaan and not to marry with them was intended to prevent idolatry and religious syncretism (Deut. 7:1–5, 20:16–18). This would be particularly crucial for the Israelites, with their developing religiously oriented culture and society, which was so prone to the influences of more developed systems. The sources of such influences were the various peoples of Canaan, the many *nachrim* (foreigners) who were constantly passing through Israel while engaged in commerce, those attached to the royal court, and those who simply settled in the land.

The *nachri* was seen by the law as an alien who was still attached to his homeland even though he lived in Israel. He did not plan to assimilate into the Israelite system, which was one in which the religious element was central, at least in the post-exilic period. While Israelite law was both civil and religious, the fact that the laws were finally cast and recorded by religionists gives them a predominantly religious flavor and motivation. This was, no doubt, seen as justified by the great number of idolatrous practices introduced, of necessity, in compliance with the terms of foreign treaties following military defeats and through intermarriages made in the national interest, the outstanding of these being Ahab's marriage to Jezebel (1 Kings 16:31).

In any event, since the *nachri* had not severed his connection with his homeland, and presumably with his native cult, he was not bound by all the laws of the host country, though discriminatory laws were directed toward him. Yet he was protected by general convention and by the traditions of the society of which he had become a part. He may best be contrasted with the *ezrach,* the native homeborn, and the *ger,* or sojourner, who, while originally a *nachri,* a foreigner within Israelite society, eventually achieved the status of *ezrach* by severing his ties with his native group and assimilating into Israelite society.

A general definition of *ger* is a foreigner who has put himself under the protection of the people among whom he is living. The usual English equivalent for *ger* is "sojourner." However, when the context seems to call for it, "stranger" is also used (Gen. 15:13: "And He said to Abram: 'Know of a surety that thy seed shall be a stranger in a land that is not theirs...'"; Exod. 2:22: "And she [Zipporah] bore a son, and he called him Gershom; for he said, 'I have been a stranger in a strange land'"). *Ger* was used in these instances to denote Hebrews, that is, Israelites, while they were yet unsettled. Subsequent to the time they settled in Canaan and formed their own polity, the term *ger* applied to non-Israelites living among them who were neither *nachrim* nor foreigners still attached to their native lands.

The definition of *ger* changed as the nature of the Israelite state changed, with the passing of time and in response to the events which took place. The biblical account seems to allow for a three-stage development. The first is where the *ger*, an immigrant, contrasted to the home-born, does not enjoy full privileges of membership in the tribe. While dependent, he is not in absolute servitude. This use of *ger* is usually found in the oldest stratum of the Pentateuch. Classical equivalents would be the *advena* and the *metic*, an alien resident in Athens who had civil privileges. As indicated above, in the period before the establishment of Israel, *ger* usually referred to Hebrews who were still not settled. Even after the beginning stages of the settlement, when the term increasingly referred to non-Israelites, Israelites were still called *gerim*.[1] This was particularly true of Levites who wandered about seeking a place for themselves (Deut. 18:6, Judg. 17:7–13). This has led at least one scholar to associate landlessness with the status of the *ger*.[2]

The next stage in the development of the term *ger* took place when a good part of the land of Israel was settled and some fixed status was necessary, not only for those who had been attached to a distant people but also for the conquered peoples of the land of Canaan. T. J. Meek finds a concern for these people in the Book of the Covenant (Exod. 20:22–23:19) and in the work of the Deuteronomist. Generally, these "resident aliens" were treated as subordinated natives who performed such tasks as wood-gathering and water-drawing (Deut. 29:10).[3] These were the tasks assigned to the Gibeonites, an indigenous people who became associated with the Israelites. During this time the *gerim* were seen to be the responsibility of Israelites no less than were orphans, widows, and slaves (Exod. 20:10, 22:20, 23:9; Deut. 5:14, 10:18, etc.). While the *gerim* were a more integral part of the Israelite community than the *nachrim,* certain ritually oriented practices did not apply to them. An animal which died naturally and therefore could not be eaten by an Israelite could be eaten by a *ger* or sold to a *nachri* (Deut. 14:21); yet at a later time, that of the Priestly edition of the Pentateuch, when the status of the *ger* changed once again, this was prohibited to the *ger* as well as the *ezrach* (Lev. 17:15).

The final development in the definition of *ger* is seen in the document known as the Holiness Code (Lev. 17–25). The material in this document is attributed to the Priestly school of the mid-sixth century B.C.E. It is during this period, according to Meek, that the Hebrew became so thoroughly identified with the land of Israel that he was called native-born and the term *ezrach* came into use. *Ger* came to mean a naturalized alien and was placed on virtually the same footing with *ezrach* in both privileges and rights. This last stage was motivated by the Priestly school's realistic appraisal of the historical situation.

During the exilic period it was necessary to keep the people together both for survival in exile and for an eventual return to Israel. According to Max Weber, the leaders of the exile utilized the religion of the people, carrying it a step further and making the Jews a ritually segregated group.[4] Additionally, while non-Israelites were still encouraged to associate themselves with the Israelites, they could no longer do so in the informal way of earlier times as *gerim* or "guest peoples" tied to a particular tribe or clan. As a result, while they would still be *gerim,* the term came to have new content. They would enter into the holy community through the act of circumcision and become a part of the ritually segregated community, or pariah people. Their center was in Jerusalem, with associated congregations elsewhere. This tendency can be seen as beginning in the late pre-exilic period.[5]

After the exile there was a dramatic failure to establish a new Israelite state with a political orientation. This is reflected in the outcome of the revolutions and insurrections led by Haggai and Zechariah early in the reign of Darius I (Hag. 2:23, Zech. 6:11). With the realization of the (at least temporary) hopelessness of a renewed kingdom, the leaders of the Jewish community accepted the status quo and turned their efforts to the development of a "church" within an empire. Survival was seen to rest upon religion. The *gerim,* whose ties to the Israelite state could in earlier times be based on both the state and the cult, would now have to be dependent on religion. Survival as a religious group would, further, have to be based on resistance to the assimilation of foreign practices.

The new Israelite group, then, had to deal with the *gerim* in its midst and with those who might join it in the future. Since the basis for affiliation could no longer be national, it became exclusively religious and cultic. With the increased importance of the cult and the priesthood, there arose another motivation for the full integration of guest peoples. When they were outside the "holy congregation," *gerim* would lend it no material support. Once "converted" to the system, they became obligated to share in the various tributes to the Temple and the priesthood; in thanksgiving offerings, especially for first fruits, firstborn, and other special occasions, in addition to the regular taxes and tribute. Also affected were those classes of Israelite society with whom the *gerim* were in direct competition. Now the *gerim,* too, would have to observe the Sabbath and other restrictions of which nonobservance had given them some advantage over the *ezrach*.[6]

Thus came into being the phenomenon of conversion although there was no formal term for the act. Further confusion of the "conversion" process resulted from the use of the same term, *ger,* for different statuses within the Israelite community. The explanation for this rests in the fact that the same terminology is used to describe very different phenomena in different periods. The *ger* went from being a simple immigrant to a resident alien to a convert to Judaism and one as loved as the *ezrach*. In this last stage he would eventually lose any stigma of ever having been a *ger* or convert.

That this sequence took place not in an evolutionary way but in response to changing historical circumstances was recognized by the translators who produced the Septuagint. Though they knew nothing of the documentary theory,* their use of different words to translate *ger* in a way fairly consistent with the explanation presented here indicates the value of contextual interpretation. For the late material, where the *ger* is treated as the *ezrach,* the Septuagint has the word προσήλυτος (i.e., proselyte, or one who has attached himself to or united or identified one-

---

* The documentary theory holds that the text of the Bible, particularly the Pentateuch, comprises materials written over a period of centuries and finally blended together by editors who fixed the text. Scholars believe that analysis of the text reveals this multiple authorship. There is considerable difference of opinion concerning the various "schools" of authors and exactly which biblical material is to be assigned to each of them.

self with an alien group) (Lev. 20:2). This word is not used in the Septuagint for *ger* in earlier material covering the first two stages. παροικέω, indicating "sojourning," is used instead. When found in material of the late state, that attributed to the Priestly school, it refers to the patriarchs in Canaan (Gen. 17:8, 35:27, 47:9; Exod. 6:4). The regular Greek term for *ger* in the early material is παροικος, which is never used for *ger* in the Priestly material except for *toshav*, "serf," which word has a meaning akin to that of *ger* in the early period (Exod. 12:45; Lev. 22:10, 25:6, 23, 35, 40, 45, 47; Num. 35:15).

During this latter period there was no question about the *ger*'s status: "One law shall be to him that is homeborn [*ezrach*] and unto the stranger [*ger*] that sojourneth among you" (Exod. 12:49). The condition sine qua non for such full equality was circumcision, the visible sign of unity with other Israelites in their covenant with God (Exod. 12:48). This equality is seen in the administration of justice (Deut. 1:16 f.) and the availability of cities of refuge (Num. 35:15), and moral and cultic obligations (Lev. 17:8, 10, 12, 13, 15, 16:29, 22:18; Num. 9:14, 15:15, 16, 29). The possibilities for the *ger* now were great: "The stranger that is in the midst of thee shall mount up above thee higher and higher; and thou shalt come down lower and lower" (Deut. 28:43). Furthermore, upon the restoration to the land of Israel, "they shall have inheritance with you among the tribes of Israel. And it shall come to pass, that in what tribe the stranger sojourneth, there shall ye give him his inheritance, saith the Lord God" (Ezek. 47:22 f.).

That the status of the *ger* was generally low may be deduced from the fact that an Israelite who becomes poor and serves as a hired servant is considered to be a *ger* (Lev. 25:39–41). It is also clear that other aliens, those who were not circumcised, did not have the status of the *ger* (Ezek. 44:9). A control distinguishing the *ger* (proselyte) from the *sachir, toshav,* and *nachri* was circumcision, which allowed him to partake of the ritual par excellence, the Passover sacrifice (Exod. 12:48, Num. 9:14). In all the passages where the *ger* is seen as equal with the *ezrach,* it is inaccurate to translate the word as "sojourner" or "stranger." The only appropriate translation is "proselyte" or "convert." In this way the *ger* in these circumstances is seen for what he is, an equal participant in the Jewish polity and religion who for the time being is recognized as one who joined himself and/or his family to the Jewish group.

Seen in this light, the prohibitions relating to intermarriage found in the books of Ezra and Nehemiah were directed not at *gerim* but at those women who had been married by Jewish men but did not convert and therefore were not assimilated into the Jewish group. The threat to both the cult and the carriers of the cult was real and had to be combatted. With this in mind, the message of Ruth is not meant to contradict Ezra and Nehemiah but merely to spell out the implications of the actions of these two men: those women who marry Jews and accept the Jewish community and its God are themselves accepted: "thy people shall be my people, and thy God my God" (Ruth 1:15).

That there was abundant intermarriage is clear (2 Chron. 30:1–12, 25). Some scholars believe that this material, placed in the time of Hezekiah (715–687) in the Bible, really applies to the time of Ezra and Nehemiah. Louis Finkelstein notes that the "plebeians" among the Jews, both in Babylonia and, later, in Judea, particularly favored accepting anyone who wished to join them.[7] They saw themselves as distinct, not for racial or national reasons, but through religion and culture. Finkelstein feels that the plebeians were generally more liberal than the other classes of the Jewish community, "favoring social justice and human equality."[8] This ideology is seen as leading to proselyting even to the extent of converting Philistines, an indication of their great zeal (Zech. 9:7). The plebeians also took a liberal view on conversion because of the difficulty they had in getting suitable wives among their fellow Jews. Being too poor to compete with middle-class Jews for Jewish women, they followed the practice of the upper class by marrying non-Jews. They married women they could afford, from among the nomadic tribes living in the grazing lands south of Judea. These were the Calebites, Jerahmeelites, and Kenites who earlier had provided male *gerim*. This very widespread practice was frightening to Ezra and was met with both the example of Ruth, who converted, and the call for putting aside those who would not join the people of Israel and their God.

It is clear that non-Israelites lived in the Jewish state, and while many of them joined themselves to the Israelites, others did not. Several problems still remain unresolved in this regard. The Rechabites (Jer. 35), while not within the Israelite genealogy, are portrayed as not only full Jews but ideal Jews. They seem to serve as the idealization of an ancient, non-Canaanite past.[9] The Gibeonites won an alliance with Joshua's invading forces and through stealth were joined to Israel, but in the subordinate roles of drawers of water and hewers of wood (Josh. 9). If they were associated with the Temple, as seems likely, then perhaps they are related to the Levites (Num. 3:9, 8:19) and the Nithinim who returned from the exile (Ezra 2:43–54, Neh. 7:46–56). They are so identified (Gibeonites and Nithinim) in a talmudic aggadic passage (*Kiddushin* 70b).[10]

The Samaritans are another problematic group. The hostility toward them is well known from Ezra and Nehemiah, and appears to have been a reaction to an attempt by the Samaritans to establish an alternate center for the Jews under the control of a group other than that represented by Ezra and Nehemiah. The Samaritans saw themselves as a remnant of the Israelites who were taken into exile when Samaria was destroyed in 722 B.C.E., augmented by some repatriated brethren fifty-five years later. They further felt that the Temple should be located on Mount Gerizim (Deut. 27:12) and that Ezra falsified the Law. The general Jewish view of the Samaritans (based on 2 Kings 17:24 ff.) is that they were descended from colonists brought by Shalmaneser from Cutha in Babylonia and Hamath after the conquest of Samaria in 722. This community was later augmented by other immigrants. It was felt that they were only partially converted, and then only through fear, but remained basically pagan.

Two possible explanations suggest themselves. First, the Samaritans represented the continuation of the old struggle between Israel and Judah. Second, the Samaritans of the mid-fifth century B.C.E. were settlers brought in from the east who sought to be independent of Jerusalem and its leadership, and to take over the leadership of Judah itself in the hope of eventually establishing their own political entity.

Solomon Zeitlin returns to the struggle between the Samaritans and Nehemiah to explain the Mishnah in *Kiddushin* 3:12 which states that the offspring of a union between a Jew and a non-Jewess is not Jewish.[11] He states that the prohibition relates to the specific historical situation confronted by Nehemiah and the Jews of the restoration in the face of the threat of the Samaritans under Sanballat to build a temple on Mount Gerizim.[12] Since this had Pentateuchal authority (Deut. 27; cf. Josh. 8:33), and the Temple in Jerusalem only historical support, it was considered essential to maintain the centrality of Jerusalem and the Jews over the Samaritans. The canonizing of the books of the Bible strengthened Jerusalem's claim to the Temple, which was based on the account in

1 Kings, stating that God chose Jerusalem for His house. In addition, this thwarted Sanballat, who sought priests for his temple by getting one of the Zadokite family to marry his daughter, thereby establishing a rival priestly dynasty (Sanballat's daughter was to marry Menassah, grandson of the high priest Eliashib; Neh. 13:28; Josephus, *Antiquities* 2. 302 f.). Since Sanballat's daughter was a Horonite, this danger was removed by the promulgation of a law that children of a non-Jewess are not Jewish.[13] In any event, the Samaritans remained an unassimilated group among the Jews. A few of them survive even today.

Although there seems to be no formal term for the process of conversion, several terms which are highly suggestive of such an act are found in the Bible. Because it has been supposed that conversion did not occur during the period covered by the Bible, any term which suggested conversion was explained by commentators and scholars as meaning something else. In fact, conversion did take place during the biblical period, and a number of words were used to describe it. The first is מתיהד (*hityahed*; Esther 8:17), used to describe the Persians who are said to have converted to Judaism from fear of the Jews, following the wondrous salvation of the Jews from Haman.[14] Whether or not the Persians were feigning to be Jews, as some conclude, the word clearly includes the idea of converting. Another term is אמילם (*'amilam*; Ps. 118:10–12), which is usually translated "I will cut them off." However, the root מול in the Bible only occurs in references to circumcision. A more likely translation would, therefore, be "All nations compassed me about: in the name of the Lord I will cause them to be circumcised."[15] In this way, through their being circumcised, God could remove the threat they posed, and thus all would join together in unity. Some relate the passages in Esther and the Psalms to the forced conversion of the Idumeans and Itureans by the Hasmoneans.[16] A final term is נלוה (*nilvah*; Isa. 56:3, 6; Zech. 2:11; Jer. 50:5; Esther 9:27). Here again the idea of conversion is clear: "Neither let the stranger, that hath joined himself to the Lord, speak, saying, 'The Lord will surely separate me from His people'" (Isa. 56:3).

There remain three categories of inhabitants in Israel which also illustrate the character of the society: the *sachir,* the *toshav,* and the *eved.* The term *sachir* seems to refer to a hired servant, whether an Israelite or a foreigner (Lev. 19:13, Deut. 24:14). In what appears to be from a later, post-exilic code, the *sachir* is noted as being neither

Israelite nor proselyte (Exod. 12:43 ff.). Here the Passover offering may be eaten by the Israelite and the circumcised servant but not the hired servant, or *sachir*. Another passage, usually dated late as well, places the poor Israelite who sells himself into bondage in the category of a hired servant who is to serve until the year of jubilee (Lev. 25:39 f.). He is not, however, actually called a *sachir* but simply serves "as" a *sachir*. While it is not possible to clearly delineate the nature of the *sachir*, it does seem that his status changed with the passing of time.

Even greater confusion exists with the term *toshav*. Part of the reason for this is its frequent use with the term *ger*. Abraham saw himself as a *ger* and *toshav*, that is, a migrant, while in Hebron seeking a burial site for Sarah (Gen. 23:4). Similarly, in two other late passages these terms are used together as referring to Israelites (Ps. 39:12, I Chron. 29:15). In another section, also usually attributed to the Holiness Code, *ger* and *toshav* are used synonymously and for both Israelites and aliens (Lev. 25:6, 23, 35, 40). In one passage *ger* is used in its verbal form for the subject *toshav* (Lev. 25:6). Yet in still another passage the Israelite, *ger*, and *toshav* are each listed separately and appear to be distinct units (Num. 35:15). It would seem, then, that *toshav* was an alternate term for *ger*, at least during the intermediate period, when the *ger* was a protected resident alien. The precise meaning was probably lost in time, though it remained in the literature.

There are biblical traditions of rather large numbers of slaves both immediately following the conquest and in the time of David and Solomon. Although the enslavement of conquered peoples eventually became prevalent as a result of the Roman and Arabic conquests, the type of society which developed earlier in Israel does not seem to have been conducive to the practice (Judg. 1:28, 30, 33, 35; 2 Chron. 2:17 f.). What seems to be more likely is that aside from the relatively few slaves owned by individuals, the conquered peoples served the general Israelite society, which was less advanced commercially and technologically than the society it conquered. The Gibeonites in some ways may have served a similar role, as well as groups such as the Philistines who had metallurgical skills unknown to the Israelites. Gradually, it may be assumed, these groups became fully identified with the Israelites as *gerim* or proselytes.

Allowance was certainly made for the *eved* to integrate himself. There were frequent marriages between Israelites and slave women, and the children of these unions took their places as freemen. In addition, the *eved* could be initiated into the Israelite cult through circumcision and then partake of the Passover offering (Exod. 12:44). This would parallel the development of the *ger,* who would eventually become a full prose-lyte equal in every way with the *ezrach.* Indeed, in one passage, slaves bought with money and slaves born in the master's house "must be cir-cumcised" (Gen. 17:12 f.). Presumably it is just this kind of *eved,* the circumcised slave, who, under certain conditions, may even inherit his master's estate (Prov. 17:2, Gen. 15:3). The individual's having been a foreigner or a slave did not prevent his becoming fully integrated into Israelite society as an equal. Regardless of the person's past life, the tendency of Israelite society was to give him full participation and equal status. In this way a relatively small group of people was able not only to conquer a territory inhabited by many peoples, but to integrate them eventually into a single society by means of initiating them into a specialized cult.

4

Ideological Underpinning for Universalism and Conversion

WHILE the legal sections of the Bible indicate something of the structure of Israelite society and its methods of dealing with and integrating non-Israelites, other parts of the Bible suggest the ideological basis of the law. Following the flood and the generations after Noah, the unity of mankind was splintered, with the implicit understanding that it would be restored at some point in history (Gen. 10:32, 11:1–9). From the time of Abraham (initially Abram) and his covenant with God, mankind would be blessed through the knowledge of God, and gradually brought back into harmony with Him and with one another. For this to be accomplished not only would immediate strangers have to be brought into the Israelite community but a world-wide mission would have to be initiated.

The *gerim* were included when the covenant was made at Sinai, and the people of God was established when it was renewed by Joshua at Gerizim and Ebal (Deut. 29:10 ff., Josh. 8:33, 35). Also mentioned in the former passage are "the hewer of thy wood and the drawer of thy water," referring, perhaps, to the Gibeonites or to the servant peoples from among those subjugated during the conquest and settlement of Canaan. Similarly, in a passage in Isaiah (56:3, 6–8):

Neither let the stranger, that hath joined himself to the Lord, speak, saying: "The Lord will surely separate me from his people"; neither let the eunuch say: "Behold, I am a dry tree." . . . Also the strangers, that join themselves to the Lord, to minister unto Him, and to love the name of the Lord, to be his servants, every one that keepeth the Sabbath from profaning it, and holdeth fast to My covenant; even them will I bring to My holy mountain, and make them joyful in My House of prayer.

28

Their burnt-offerings and their sacrifices shall be accepted upon My altar: for My house shall be called a house of prayer for all peoples. The Lord God, which gathereth the outcasts of Israel, saith: "Yet I gather others to him, beside his own that are gathered."

The general call for open and full acceptance seems clear here. However as noted toward the end of the last passage cited from Isaiah, not only were the immediate neighbors to be included. In his Temple address, Solomon declares, "That all the peoples of the earth may know that the Lord, he is God; there is none else" (1 Kings 8:60; cf. 2 Kings 19:15).

While the following by no means includes all of the passages which contain the "vision" of Israel, they do indicate the general content of the message.[1]

. . . and all nations shall flow unto [the Lord's house]. And many peoples . . . will walk in His paths: for out of Zion shall go forth the law and the word of the Lord from Jerusalem (Isa. 2:2 f.).

And the stranger shall join himself with them [Jacob and Israel], and they shall cleave unto the house of Jacob (Isa. 14:1).

That they may know from the rising of the sun, and from the west, that there is none beside Me: I am the Lord, and there is none else (Isa. 45:6).

For then I will turn to the peoples a pure language, that they may all call upon the name of the Lord, to serve Him with one consent (Zeph. 3:9).

All the ends of the earth shall remember and turn unto the Lord: and all the kindreds of the nations shall worship before Thee. For the kingdom is the Lord's; and He is ruler over the nations (Ps. 22:28).

O sing unto the Lord a new song: sing unto the Lord, all the earth. Sing unto the Lord, bless His name, show forth His salvation from day to day. Declare His glory among the nations, His marvelous works among all the peoples (Ps. 96:1–3).

In addition, of course, there is the Book of Jonah with its concern for the salvation of the gentiles. Not only are all peoples to be brought to God, but the people of Israel, beginning with Abraham and following through his descendants, are to have a special role in this process. Nations and peoples are to come and be blessed through Abraham (Gen. 12:2, 17:1–7, 22:17 f.). Jeremiah as an individual was "appointed . . . a prophet unto the nations" (Jer. 1:5). But so was all Israel: "I the Lord . . . give thee for a covenant of the people, for a light of the gentiles" (Isa. 42:6).

This mission was to be carried on with the understanding that it would be difficult and would cause suffering for those engaged in it (Isa. 52:13–53:12). According to Max Weber, this welcoming of the stranger was related to the increased status of the Jews in Persia once they began to attain high court offices, joined with the prophetic teachings which provided the motivation for survival as a specialized group, distinguished by particular rituals (making them a "pariah" people), permitting the people to remain loyal to God, who allowed them to suffer, fail, and be enslaved. With the prophetic rationale, they worshipped their God even more ardently. Weber sees this as a great paradox: the high self-image of the Jews led them to seek and win converts.[2]

A radically different approach is taken by Harry Orlinsky. He feels that "it is almost beyond comprehension how the plain meaning of this chapter [Isa. 49] is sometimes subverted by the 'universalists' in order to attribute to the prophet the idea of the restoration of Israel, the conversion of the heathen nations and the final status of the Jews and Gentiles in God's kingdom."[3] Orlinsky contends that the usually accepted view—that the prophet's message propounds an internationalism which has never been achieved—is based on reading into the message ideas that developed more than half a millennium later.[4] In Orlinsky's reading, the prophet is utterly nationalistic. His only concern was the rescue which had been promised to Israel, and he was not interested in extending God's salvation to the ends of the earth. The servant about whom the prophet was speaking did not seek to be a light to the peoples but rather a light to guide every Israelite wanderer home. His mission was to gather in the exiles wherever they might be scattered. Second Isaiah's only purpose was to proclaim the deliverance of the Judean people. Orlinsky's central thesis is that whatever a particular people do, they do for themselves, although verbiage may be used to conceal their self-interest. While this is certainly a valid general interpretation, he apparently fails to see how the idea of bringing all nations to God and individuals and groups into Judaism could also serve the particular interests of Israel.

The phenomenon of conversion, not formally articulated but widely practiced nonetheless, was an ever-increasing one during the biblical period. It helped assimilate conquered peoples as well as those who came to live within the Israelite polity. During and after the exile, when it appeared that there would no longer be a Jewish state, conversion continued with the old motivation but with a new aspect as well. Not only would it serve to bring born gentiles into the Jewish group, but it would help Judaism to survive by compensating for the dramatic losses suffered through the destruction of the state and later while in exile. So strong was this drive that the exilic literature was filled with statements indicating the universality of Judaism. This universality had its particularistic side in that non-Jews were expected to formally align themselves with Judaism through an act which long after the biblical period was to be called "conversion." That the universalist sentiments expressed in the Bible were later used for different purposes— as arguments encouraging the unity of all mankind and supporting political schemes like the League of Nations, the United Nations, or federal world government—should not blind us to the special use of these ideas in the unique situation in which the Jews found themselves two and a half millennia ago.

PART II
THE RABBINIC PERIOD

5
Historical Background

CONVERSION, which developed during the biblical period as a religious act with political and social purposes, became a highly formalized and articulated ritual during the rabbinic period. This development was a continuation of, rather than a sharp break from, the past. Changed conditions and greater awareness of the past made it both possible and necessary. While the biblical period ends in the mid-fifth century B.C.E. with the events recounted in the books of Ezra and Nehemiah, modern critical scholars date several other sections of the Bible as late as the Maccabean period, in the second century B.C.E. The books of Esther, Job, and Ecclesiastes, as well as many Psalms, are dated after Ezra and Nehemiah.

For the purposes of this study, the rabbinic period will be dated from the second century B.C.E. until the rise of Islam in the seventh century C.E. While our major concern is the development of the idea of conversion in Judaism, our thesis is that the concept developed only in response to specific historical circumstances. Indeed, one may anticipate or describe particular historical conditions from a knowledge of the attitude and practice of conversion by Jews at any particular time. In other words, the phenomenon of conversion may be seen as one of the basic controls which may be used in the study of Jewish history. It is particularly suited for this role since it is one of the social devices utilized within the Jewish community from its initial entrance into human history. The actual awareness of this came in the rabbinic period, when Abraham was seen as the first convert to the one, true God and whose role it was, together with his wife and family, to bring all mankind to this same God and the religion which embodied the worship of Him.

The Jewish literature of this period is extensive and, as was true with the biblical material, much of it cannot be precisely dated. It includes

35

the Mishnah, which is a compilation of much of the law and lore of the period from approximately 200 B.C.E. through 180 C.E. Additional material from the same period that was not included in the Mishnah can be found in the Tosefta. Similar material, which developed in both Babylonia and Palestine and was compiled some 250 years later, forms, together with the Mishnah, the great multi-volume work known as the Talmud. In addition, there are various collections of homiletical materials based on the Bible, known as Midrashim, which span this entire period. Finally, there are the works of the Jewish general and historian, Josephus; the works of biblical interpretation and philosophy of Philo of Alexandria, and the Apocrypha and Pseudepigrapha. Materials from Greek and Roman authors are also helpful in reconstructing the Jewish experience in this period.

During the 800-year span covered in this section, the Middle East as usual was extremely dynamic. Empires rose and fell, and with them great cultural traditions. While empires vanished in the face of more dynamic peoples, something of the cultures they had developed usually remained. The Greek, Persian, and Roman empires were so vast that their cultural impact included not only their own indigenous cultures but elements from the whole range of dominated peoples. Communication and travel also increased, further enhancing cultural interchange. Greek culture became a permanent part of the eastern shore of the Mediterranean with the grand sweep of Alexander the Great in the fourth century B.C.E. He and his armies conquered as far east as India as well as into Egypt. After the decline of Alexander's successors, the known world was divided between a resurgent Persian Empire in the east and the Romans in the west. After many centuries the Romans and the Persians were replaced by the Arabs, who in less than one hundred years took control of a vast swath of land including Spain, all of North Africa, the Middle East, Central Asia and parts of the Far East. While bringing little in the way of culture other than their religion, which itself was principally derivative of Judaism and Christianity, they introduced a new common language and cultural base which served to bring together the many cultural strands found within their empire. During this same period, many philosophies and religions competed for the minds, hearts, and loyalties of the millions who lived in the Mediterranean world. Even the philosophies and religions that failed and died out, such as Stoicism, Epicureanism, and the mystery cults, left their impact upon those that survived. Judaism, one of the survivors, helped to spawn two new world faiths, Christianity and Islam, which threatened to swamp and even destroy her.

That Judaism survived this period is accounted by many a miracle. A question less often asked is, why did she not become the world faith instead of her children, Christianity and Islam? Once again the key may be found in Judaism's practice of conversion, the path to survival which Jews developed, and the kind of social phenomenon they saw themselves to be. The Jewish people entered this period as dependents of the Persian Empire. Following the failure of the successors of Alexander the Great to hold his empire together either in toto or in segments, a new Jewish state established itself under the Hasmoneans, who ruled briefly, from 165 to 63 B.C.E. However, Rome reinstated foreign rule over Palestine. The Romans were followed by the Arabs. No Jewish state was to be reestablished until 1948.

The Jewish pattern of survival as a religious polity without political aspirations, a pattern begun during the exile after the destruction of the Jewish state in 586 B.C.E., and developed in Judea during the time from Ezra and Nehemiah until the Hasmonean period, reasserted itself once again. This pattern, embellished during the period of the development of the Talmud, was to become the normative Judaism of the subsequent millennia. Jewish leaders saw the Jewish people as a holy enclave, the carriers of a divine message. The people and the message were to be kept pure at all costs in the face of dramatic political and cultural threats. If the world could not now be converted to the truth, this truth and its carrier would be protected and maintained until God in His wisdom and mercy delivered them. Meanwhile, neither the message nor the mission was to be abandoned.

During this period, once Christianity was established as the state religion of the Roman Empire, proselyting and conversion became capital offenses. After the area came under Islamic domination, they were virtually impossible. During this time the Jewish mission began to enter its quiescent stage. Yet before Christianity was established in the Roman realm, and Islam in the Arabic domain, several mass conversions took place. While some discussion of these will be included here, extensive descriptions will be given in later chapters. One of these mass conversions followed the pattern set in the biblical period. Conquering Jewish armies under the Hasmoneans, about 120–95 B.C.E., gave dominated peoples the option of accepting Judaism or leaving their land. The centuries-old method of consolidating conquered populations was asserted as soon as the opportunity and necessity were presented.

Another kind of mass conversion during this period came not through coercion by dominant Jewish imperial force but through the convictions of large numbers of individuals. This kind of mass conversion took place with great frequency throughout the Roman Empire. A similar kind of conversion seems to have taken place among the Berbers in Northwest Africa in the pre-Islamic period. Furthermore, the leaders of two nations, and perhaps their peoples as well, converted during this period, apparently both out of conviction and in order to resolve specific social and political problems. These were the Adiabeneans of northern Mesopotamia in the first century C.E., and the southern Arabians, led by Dhu Nuwas, in the fifth century C.E.

Dramatic population changes among the Jews in Palestine and the diaspora are attributed partially to the great number of proselytes. According to one scholar, the Jewish population of Palestine increased from 20,000–40,000 immediately after the Exile, to 200,000 before the expansion under the Hasmoneans, to 2,500,000 by the year 70 C.E.[1] Adding to this the number of Jews in the diaspora, some scholars believe the Jews to have been one of the most significant groups in the region. Salo Baron estimates the Jewish population during the Roman period as 8,000,000. There were a million or more each in Syria, Egypt, Babylonia, and Asia Minor, triple the number of Jews in Palestine.[2] While the Jews comprised 10 percent of the population of the Roman Empire, in the most advanced Hellenistic sector of the eastern Mediterranean, they were 20 percent.[3]

Both Baron and Joseph Klausner state that this increase is attributable primarily to proselytism. Other factors might include high natural increase aided by advanced hygienic rules. Similar reasons were advanced by Josephus, who lived during the period, while Philo, perhaps overimpressed by the large Jewish population of his hometown, Alexandria, believed that half the human race was Jewish.[4]

These high estimates for the Roman period are particularly amazing in the light of the two great defeats suffered by the Jews in the first century C.E. The brutal and costly crushing of the Jewish uprising in 70 brought an end to the Second Temple and Jewish political aspirations. Compensations were essential for survival. The religious center gradually moved to Babylonia, and conversion was encouraged even more than previously to build numbers. Jews were now scattered more than before, both out of necessity and through the openness of the Roman Empire. This made the possibilities for proselyting greater than they had been. Proselytization was not carried out by professional missionaries but rather by itinerant preachers and rhetoricians, the influence of Jewish merchants, and vigorous propaganda. The spread of Hellenism and the Roman administrative system tended to break down many barriers among the various peoples of the empire, allowing Judaism, together with the many other religions and philosophies of the time, to compete for the minds and hearts of the peoples. A further motivation for a proselyting campaign by Jews was the growing aggressiveness of evangelistic Christianity, spurred by Paul and directed primarily toward Jews in its earliest stages. The best defense against this challenge may well have been seen to be a counterdrive for converts.[5]

6

Proselytization and the Rabbis

FOR GENERATIONS Jewish and gentile scholarship, reflecting the attitudes toward proselytizing which had developed in the preceding several centuries, maintained that Judaism was generally hostile to the seeking and winning of converts. This attitude, which grew out of the restrictions in the Christian and Islamic milieus, was read back into Jewish history. George Foot Moore, Bernard J. Bamberger, and William G. Braude have done much to dispel this view for the rabbinic period. With a wealth of examples from the totality of rabbinic literature, Bamberger has illustrated that the rabbis were overwhelmingly favorable to both conversion and converts. He believes Moore's earlier remark, that "the tone of the utterances about proselytes is friendly though not unduly enthusiastic," [1] is an understatement. Bamberger can find only one statement which is clearly hostile to converts, while three others appear to be hostile but are somewhat obscure. A few others are directed not against converts as such but against insincere proselytes.[2]

According to rabbinic tradition, the first Hebrew was a convert to monotheism. Furthermore, Abraham was then to embark on the life of a missionary and seeker of converts. He was to convert the men, and Sarah the women. The dispersion of Israel, the result of the destruction of the Jewish kingdoms, was frequently seen as a punishment for disloyalty to God. But it was also viewed as part of God's salvationist scheme. "The Holy One, blessed be He, dispersed the people of Israel among the nations in order that they might acquire proselytes" (*Pesachim* 87b). Rabbi Hoshiah said that "God acted righteously toward Israel when He scattered them among the nations." [3] Another statement notes that the proselyte is dearer to God than the Israelite, since he has

40

come of his own accord while the Israelites came as a result of the miracles exhibited at Mount Sinai.[4] Resh Lakish noted that the person who oppresses the convert is as one who has oppressed God (*Hagigah* 5a; based on Mal. 3:5). It is never too late for a person to convert. To teach this Abraham did not enter the covenant until he was ninety-nine, when he was circumcised. As with Abraham, so every Israelite has the obligation to bring men under the "wing of the *Shechinah*."[5] The many marriages of Solomon to foreign women, which could have been condemned, were viewed as having the purpose of making them love God and converting to belief in Him.[6] While some rabbinic opinions hold that those who become proselytes out of love for a Jew or out of fear or for worldly gain are not to be received, the law is according to Rav, who stated that they are to be considered proselytes and to receive friendly treatment since there is the possibility that they did convert out of pure motives.[7]

The general goal of the rabbis was to bring "all men under the wings of the *Shechinah*."[8] The conviction of the Jews that theirs was the one true religion, from which it would follow that all should eventually come to it, was a unique development. "No other religion in their world and time made any such pretensions or cherished such aspirations."[9] In contrast was the general tolerance of pagan religions. In the same way most imperial regimes allowed peoples to follow their own rites. While it seems that missionaries were not dispatched specifically to win converts, the presence of Jews and their institutions throughout the Mediterranean world had a great effect.[10] Braude feels, on the other hand, that seminaries or academies might have been established in larger centers to spread learning not only to Jews but to gentiles as well. Rabbis Judah and Joseph, heads of the great school in Pumpeditha, censured certain communities for their failure to attract sufficient numbers of proselytes. A century later, Rabbi Ashi (352–427) made a similar complaint against the Jews of Mata Mahseia, a suburb of the other great Babylonian center of Sura on the Euphrates.[11]

One of the most discussed passages regarding Jewish proselytism during this period is Matthew 23:15: "Woe unto you, scribes and Pharisees, hypocrites! for ye compass sea and land to make one proselyte; and when he is become so, ye make him twofold more a son of hell than yourselves." From this passage one could conclude not only that the rabbis traveled far as active and intensive missionaries, but that their converts became extremely zealous. Contrary to the usual interpretation, this passage simply verifies the testimony of other contemporary Jewish and gentile sources: the official leaders of Judaism "were eager to make converts, were highly successful in winning them, and friendly in their treatment of them." [12] Proselyting went on in the biblical period and accelerated "both in scope and intensity after the Maccabean victories." [13] This movement was implemented by extensive propaganda literature as well as personal missionary effort, official and otherwise. Braude, however, believes that the passage in Matthew refers to zeal for the individual convert. He does not find any evidence for formal conversionist schemes either through missionaries or propaganda literature. [14]

Negative attitudes and even hostility toward converts were not uncommon at this time. They were outgrowths of both general conditions and specific historical events. Many persons who were born Jewish simply felt superior to those who came in through conversion. Some racialism does seem to have existed. Moore explains this clearly: "Equality in law and religion does not necessarily carry with it complete social equality, and the Jews would have been singularly unlike the rest of mankind if they had felt no superiority to their heathen converts." [15] Further, large numbers of converts would not only threaten the status of born Jews but would also compete for community positions and honors. While conversion might be in the interests of the "religious establishment" as a means of increasing the number of its adherents, this increase could be viewed as a mixed blessing by the laity. This is seen in the many statements holding that those who convert out of fear, or for marriage, or to serve the king, or to take part in the messianic age, are not true converts. [16]

Negative attitudes may also have been directed toward converts who did not wholly commit themselves to Judaism as well as those who slipped back to their former pagan beliefs. Josephus takes note of the great number of Greeks who observed Jewish law but then departed from it (*Against Apion* 2. 123). [17] Among the Eighteen Blessings of the worship service is a special blessing for true or sincere proselytes, apparently in recognition of this problem. [18] There also seems to have been a large group of half-proselytes who may have aroused a special animus. They were variously called "devout ones," "God-fearers," and "worshippers of God." [19] Klausner believes that many of the hostile statements were directed against these people, who accepted "the loftier ideas of Judaism such as monotheism and the ethics of the prophets," observed "the Sabbath and refrained from eating swine's flesh but they did not observe the numerous ritual rules of Pharisaic Judaism." [20]

The destruction of the Temple, Christian competition and then persecution, the defection of some converts, the failure of the Bar Kochba revolt in 135 C.E., and the intensified group loyalty fostered by the misfortunes of this period, little influenced attitudes and restrictions regarding conversion. While some negative elements did enter the Halachah (Law), the Aggadah (homiletics) remained firmly friendly toward converts. It is related that Rabbi Simon ben Yochai, in spite of being betrayed to the Roman authorities by the son of a convert during the Hadrianic persecutions for his antagonism to Rome and his persistent study of the Jewish holy books, taught that the convert is dearer to God than the person born Jewish.[21] To obviate the admission of uncommitted converts and those who were spies for Rome, a more rigorous procedure was instituted for questioning and training converts (*Yevamot* 47b).

Increased suspicion and even hostility did not curb the continuous process of proselyting and conversion. The attitude toward converts may also be seen in the various laws regarding intermarriage and officeholding by proselytes. In respect to the former, those within the priestly ranks felt that the long tradition of purity was to be maintained, particularly by the priestly families. Also, since many offices required a full understanding of religious law, there was concern over the qualifications of the convert. The danger of syncretism and of being swamped by insincere and uninformed converts was of great concern.[22] What may often appear to be restrictive was often precautionary. Some elements of Jewish society, notably the Sadducees and some extreme nationalists, were no doubt hostile. They would withhold full Jewish status even from those who were third-generation converts. Thus, the grandson of Herod, Agrippa I, was not considered a full-fledged Judean.[23]

A similar problem was confronted in the social-class and ancestral tests for public and judicial offices. The rabbis gradually and steadily reduced the qualifications, such as ancestral requirements, to having a Jewish mother and father. The problem became more difficult and complicated in the case of the priests, whose aristocracy claimed a history of 1,500 years. Blood purity was particularly important to them, and marriage with pagan women was always suspect because of their assumed loose morality.[24] However, a serious problem was the question of how many generations it took for a Jewish descendent of a convert to be really acceptable. For the average Israelite this was of no concern, conversion apparently usually following marriage. This was particularly true of the lower classes, as has been seen. The rigid prohibitions against mixing with heathens detailed in the Talmud (*Avoda Zara*) had as their underlying motive not exclusiveness or unsociability but self-preservation. These prohibitions, relating to eating, drinking, and having social intercourse with gentiles, would often lead to animus.

The prohibitions against marrying gentiles were motivated by a combination of factors: racial purity, cultural exclusiveness, preservation of the religion. This part of the Deuteronomic reformation reached a high point at the time of Ezra. As the Palestinian Jewish community became more secure and large numbers of proselytes came into Judaism, these prohibitions had less effect, though they returned under conditions similar to those which motivated them originally. Throughout, however, the tension between the universalism of the prophets and the tradition of racial exclusiveness of the priests continued. Even while the tradition of racial purity continued, the proselyte upon conversion was considered a newborn child and, for most practical purposes, equal to born Jews.[25]

When the motivation of racial purity declined as an instrument to prevent marriage with gentiles, national preservation and then group solidarity became the operative factors.[26] Gentiles were acceptable as marriage partners upon conversion, although frequently the conversion was subsequent to the intention to marry or to the marriage itself. The decreasing racial factor is seen in the development of the Pharisaic law, where originally a minimum of three generations of Hebrew ancestry were necessary to gain the status of a native Jew. The requirement was reduced to two generations and then one. Finally, the sole requirement was that at least one parent must be a native Jew. Such a person could then be king of the Jewish people, judge of any court, and holder of any responsible community office. Slowly the Pharisees even forced this teaching on the priests in their marriage laws. Again the process was gradual, until eventually a girl with one native Jewish parent was acceptable as the bride of a priest. The Halachah went even farther, permitting marriage between a priest and a girl whose parents were both proselytes, but this lenient law was not followed.

The tension between universalism and particularism was constant. Both were ideologies for survival. One would maintain the integrity of the group, the other provided for cultural and physical growth. At times one was more appropriate for survival and group health and so would prevail. Certainly they could be neither separated neatly nor interchanged. They overlapped, and the health of the community could be maintained by whatever balance was required at the moment. When the community felt itself under siege, it would withdraw, as during the period of Ezra and Nehemiah. When it was a self-conscious community, sure of its identity and secure in its position, it felt itself capable of assimilating outsiders with impunity. The more open the Jewish society became under the impact of Hellenism, the greater was the danger of its being totally swamped. Laws were necessary to alleviate this.

The Hasmonean triumph was also helpful in defining the Jewish community as a historical-political-religious one, which could continue to welcome converts without great danger of losing its character. With the support of a state, the policy toward possible converts could even be liberalized, as can be seen by the teachings of Hillel and other talmudic rabbis. The danger was the disappearance of the special Jewish identity. Where there seemed to be little chance of this, marriage with gentiles was adequately provided for.[27]

When Jewish racial components weakened, other factors were utilized to maintain group identity. First, the convert was considered a newborn. Then every manner of ritual and cultic practice was invented to give content to his new identity and to maintain that of the native Jew. The openness of the rabbis to converts was paralleled by this ritual development, which pervaded every aspect of life from birth through death. Encouragement of conversion greatly stimulated racial mingling of every variety with native Jews.[28] At the same time, Judaism saw itself as composed of a particular people especially characterized by a special religion. The convert simultaneously joined both the religion and the people, and this factor may have limited Judaism's success in attracting converts, since they were expected to join themselves to the entirety of a cultural system. Judaism was relatively less successful than either Christianity or Islam due to both its demands on converts and its failure in generating or joining a powerful imperium. It did, however, set a basic procedure which Christianity and Islam could improve.

Whatever growth Judaism had came from its converts. Realistically,

Judaism understood that it could not challenge Roman power. This was particularly so after the failures of the rebellions of 70 and 135. In addition, the Pharisaic teachings of universalism, salvation, and merit through good deeds favored the diaspora, where most Jews then lived. Not only was Palestine no longer the center, it was not necessary for the survival of the Jewish people. Legitimizing proselytes legitimated diaspora Jewry. For this reason Hillel, who was from Babylonia, made conversion as easy as possible, as did most of the rabbis of the region. Another motivating factor for proselyting may have been the commercial interests of the more liberal element. These would benefit from widespread diaspora communities which could serve as depots, as sources of reliable monetary exchange, and as agents with a common language and basic trust in one another.

In their own state the Israelites had utilized their special religion and its rituals to assimilate peoples among whom they settled and conquered. Once they became a dispersed people, or even a people living in its own land when it was dominated by outsiders, they utilized the same system to maintain their integrity and identity. Gentiles continued to be welcome within the system, which had, under the rabbis, become more formalized than during the biblical period. Max Weber's formulation of the "pariah" or "guest" people is most helpful here. Weber used it, not as a term of approbation, but to describe a "ritually segregated guest people." [29] During the early period of the settlement, there could be peoples rather loosely associated with the Israelites. Late in the pre-exilic period it became necessary for the affiliation to be completed through circumcision, which earned full equality with native-born Israelites. Conversion accelerated with the growth of the diaspora and the greater dependency upon factors other than a national state to hold the people together. The very prohibition against mixed marriage itself promoted conversion as an essential requisite for marriage to gentiles. [30] The Jews took on their pariah-people character voluntarily. It often appeared to be a rejection of the outside community, and it may be seen as part of the origin of anti-Semitism, but this was a price which had to be paid for the kind of exclusivism which the Jewish system seemed to demand. It was a price Jews willingly paid to carry on what they believed to be a divinely ordained mission. But at no point was the Jewish group closed to gentiles. Openness to converts, on the contrary, grew to its greatest heights just when the ritual system was expanded and detailed into every aspect of life.

7

Other Jewish Voices Favoring Proselyting

SOME scholars believe that much of the other material and institutions of this period were developed primarily for the purposes of Jewish propaganda directed toward winning converts. The synagogue itself, central for the worship of God by Jews, was considered especially attractive by pagans who sought religious truth and inspiration. Even the translation of the Bible into Greek had the winning of converts as one of its functions.[1] Translation was also necessary for many Jews of Alexandria and elsewhere, since they could not read Hebrew. Propagandizing gentiles was a primary function of other works of this time, including the Sybilline Oracles and the books of Judith and Tobit.[2]

The works of Philo and Josephus illustrate a deep interest in explaining Judaism to gentiles—in part, at least, to open the doors to possible conversion. Josephus' status among Jews is rather low because of his defection to the Romans during the war of 70 C.E. Yet his works are the only Jewish eyewitness historical account of the time. And he seems to have been convinced of the worth of Judaism. "The consideration given by our legislator [Moses] to the equitable treatment of aliens also merits attention. It will be seen that he took the best of all possible measures at once to secure our own customs from corruption, and to throw them open ungrudgingly to any who elect to share them. To all who desire to come and live under the same laws with us, he gives a gracious welcome, holding that it is not family ties alone which constitute relationship, but agreement in the principles of conduct. On the other hand, it was his pleasure that casual visitors should be admitted to the intimacies of our daily life" (*Against Apion* 2. 210).

This openness is compared to the traditions of the Greeks—in this instance the Spartans, who made a practice of expelling foreigners and not allowing their own citizens to travel abroad. "They might be justly reproached for discourtesy, because they accorded no one the rights either of citizenship or of residence among them. We, on the contrary, while we have no desire to emulate the customs of others, yet gladly welcome any who wish to share our own. That, I think, may be taken as a proof both of humanity and magnanimity" (*Against Apion* 2. 261). Many Greeks seem to have joined. "From the Greeks we are severed more by our geographical position than by our institutions, with the result that we neither hate nor envy them. On the contrary, many of them have agreed to adopt our laws; some of whom have remained faithful, while others, lacking the necessary endurance, have again seceded" (ibid. 123 f.). And more: "The masses have long since shown a keen desire to adopt our religious observances; and there is not one city, Greek or barbarian, nor a single nation, to which our custom of abstaining from work on the seventh day has not spread, and where the fasts and the lighting of lamps and many of our prohibitions in the matter of food are not observed" (ibid. 282). How widespread conversion to Judaism was in some locales is seen from Josephus' account of the slaughter of the Jews of Damascus. Because most of their wives had converted to Judaism, the men of Damascus plotted against the Jews secretly, refraining from informing their wives of their plans (*Jewish War* 2. 559–61).

For Philo, a proselyte was one who had resolved to change to the true religion and become naturalized in a new and godly commonwealth. Renouncing their mythical fictions, proselytes adhered to the unadulterated truth in the form of the Law of Moses. They would enjoy equal rights in every respect with the native born. Special hospices were to be established for the reception of aspirants for conversion. Erwin Goodenough, among other scholars, believes that many of Philo's writings were directed toward converting gentiles.[3] This is seen particularly in *De Vita Mosis*. Here it seems that Philo is not concerned, as he is in some of his similar works, with refuting attacks on the Jews. It is rather a polemic and an elementary introduction to the ideals of Judaism for interested outsiders, using the story of Moses and the establishment of the Jewish law as its base.[4] Proselytes are highly praised as equals of Jews and worthy of the rights and privileges of the chosen race.[5] Since many of the ideas in this work would not have been of interest to Jews and might have been alien to them, Goodenough concludes that it was specifically for gentiles. Perhaps it may have been for God-fearers or those already somewhat disposed to conversion.[6]

8

The Process of Conversion and the Convert's Status

THE HISTORY of the development of conversion is complicated somewhat by the fact that certain biblical terms were given new meanings in the rabbinic period, reflecting the special needs of the later era. Thus, for the Rabbis a *ger* was a full convert to Judaism. A *ger toshav* was a resident alien who was permitted to live in Jewish territory on the condition that he not engage in the worship of other gods or in idolatrous practices, not blaspheme the name of God, be subject to the jurisdiction of the established courts, not engage in flagrant crimes, homicide, robbery, theft, incest, and adultery, and abstain from eating flesh with the life-blood in it. In other words, he was obligated to observe the seven Noachite laws, which were said to have been given by God to Noah and were binding upon all "righteous" gentiles. The *ger toshav* was not required to join in the worship of God or to observe any of the obligations of Israel toward God. He enjoyed the exemption from labor on the Sabbath. That he was not a proselyte is seen from the facts that he could eat carrion, which no Israelite or proselyte might touch, and that charging him interest was allowed.

Several terms came into usage for the proselyte or *ger*. A proselyte who converted out of purely religious motivation was called a *ger tsedek*, or righteous proselyte. He might also be called *ger emet*, a true or genuine proselyte, or *ger ben b'rit*, a partner in the covenant. This would distinguish him from the person who converted for some other reason, such as marriage or fear, or for some material advantage. Such *gerim* would remain legally proselytes and fully protected by the law. Among these were the Gibeonites. The term *ger shaar*, proselyte of the gate, has been erroneously thought to signify a half-proselyte. It does not appear in any rabbinic source but is based on Exodus 20:10: "the stranger who is in thy gates."[1] There were no semi-proselytes in the legal sense, and only approximating this would be the *ger toshav*, the foreigner who lived in Judea who had to observe the Noachite laws.[2]

Somewhat associated with the formal convert, or *ger*, is the category variously known as "God-fearers," "devout ones," and "worshippers of God." They are mentioned in the Psalms, in Josephus, and in the Acts of the Apostles. Most of them kept the Sabbath and appropriated the loftier ideas of Judaism, such as monotheism and the ethics of the prophets. They refrained from eating pig's flesh, but did not observe the numerous other ritual rules of Rabbinic Judaism. They were neither proselytes nor half-proselytes but simply gentiles who ceased to worship any foreign deity and kept certain Jewish observances which were agreeable to them.[3] Zeitlin, however, believes that they were pagans who continued to worship their own gods yet feared and revered the God of Israel.[4] Further confusion enters the terminology because "fearers of heaven" was not a technical term for any particular group of proselytes but may have referred to pagans who abstained from idol worship, recognizing the God of the universe as the only God.[6]

These semi-proselytes are identified in the Greek and Latin by the terms *sebomenoi*, or *phoboumenoi ton theon* and *metuentes*. For want of a better English term they have been called semi-proselytes, although Wolfson calls them "spiritual proselytes."[7] Ralph Marcus regards these "fearers of heaven" as gentile sympathizers who identified in some ways with Judaism.[8] Philo simply identifies them as a third category of proselytes who had renounced idolatry and led virtuous lives. He included in this category gentiles who had nothing to do with Judaism but who in their own way, through the power of reason, had arrived at a philosophical concept of God and a philosophy calling for a life of virtue. Among these were the Magi of Persia and the Gymnosophists of India, and such individuals as Plato, Aristotle, and the outstanding Stoics. In the messianic age they would be considered full proselytes.[9]

Only gradually did formal rituals become necessary for initiation into Judaism. Rabbinic literature calls for circumcision for males and baptism and an offering in the Temple for both males and females. Earlier it appears that no ceremony was necessary. Ruth simply makes a declaration of loyalty, and Hillel instructs the pagan to go and study. Zeitlin holds that circumcision was not necessary for conversion but was performed following conversion to fulfill the obligation of being a Jew. This would hold with the discussion of the necessity of the Adiabenean prince's circumcision. Following the destruction of the Second Temple, circumcision became imperative to indicate acceptance of Judaism and the persecution attendant to it.[10] Yet if uncircumcised the convert was still considered a Jew, but "changed except for one item" (*Hulin* 4b). Zeitlin also states that baptism became a part of the ritual only after 65 C.E., when all non-Jews were declared ipso facto unclean.[11] Baptism was not a part of the act of conversion but was the cleansing necessary so that conversion could take place. Similarly, the sacrifice of two doves in the Temple was not part of the conversion ritual, but to end the status of being unclean (Lev. 12:6–8, 15:4).[12]

Originally, Zeitlin writes further, the term used for "convert" in rabbinic literature was the Hebrew *mumar,* or "changer." This person was one who had changed his god for the God of Israel. He was also a changer of his law (*dat*). Josephus records that Epiphanes, son of King Antiochus, refused to marry Drusilla, the daughter of King Agrippa, because he did not want to change to the Jewish law (*Jewish Antiquities* 20. 139). He also notes that Helena and Izates of Adiabene, as well as Sylleus, the son of King Bodas of Arabia, who wanted to marry Salome, the sister of King Herod, "changed their way of life, accepting the Judean customs and laws" (*Jewish Antiquities* 16. 225 and 20. 38; Ἰουδαίων ἔθεσιν). Similarly a Jew who forsook his religion and accepted the Hellenistic way of life was also called a *mumar.* Of Dositheus, who was born a Jew but became a Hellene, Third Maccabees uses the phrase, "he changed his laws" (1:3). Zeitlin believes that after the fall of the Judean state, or shortly before, the term *ger* came to be used for a convert to Judaism while *mumar* was retained for one who had forsaken Judaism.[13]

Another category without any special legal prescriptions is *gerurim,* converts brought into Judaism through improper motives. These would include the Gibeonites, who entered through guile, and the Idumeans and Itureans, who were forcibly intimidated into conversion. Of course, their status under Jewish law was not affected.[14] Josephus did not apply the term *ethnos* to either the Idumeans or the Adiabeneans, indicating that they did not assimilate with the native Jews so as to become one ethnic group with them but continued to live as separate nations or entities. The Idumeans considered themselves a kindred nation, perhaps because of the tradition that they were children of Edom (Esau), and because they intermarried with the Judeans. Josephus calls them *homophulon,* which Zeitlin translates as "co-religionists," not "kinsmen" as Thackeray translates it (*Jewish War* 1. 5 f.). In line with this, Herod's descendants were considered full Jews although neither his father nor his mother was a native Jew.[15] Agrippa, his grandson, read from the Torah on Sukkot. Actually, during the Second Commonwealth, because of the great number of converts, there was not a Jewish race but, rather, a Jewish people. Even the peoples prohibited by biblical law from marrying Jews, including the Ammonites, who were excluded forever, were allowed to intermarry and convert. This was allowed by the Tannaim (rabbis of the Mishnah) on the theory that, after Sennacherib mingled the nations during his wars, there were no pure races.[16]

While proselytes had full legal status, the Halachah (legal section of the Talmud) considered them a fourth estate after the Kohanim, Leviim, and Israelim. Within this framework, they too would be prohibited from marrying those forbidden to enter the congregation of Israel (Deut. 23:9; *Tos. Kiddushin* 5:1). In another legal listing, the *ger* is placed after the *mamzer* (bastard), though he would be in a more privileged position regarding marriage. Technically the *ger* could not marry a priest or hold public office although in practice these prohibitions were changed.[17]

9
The Greco-Roman Environment

ALEXANDER THE GREAT'S invasion of the eastern shore of the Mediterranean and the area from India to Egypt in the middle of the fourth century led to European domination of the area for one thousand years. The Greeks were followed by the Romans. Together they unsettled old empires, dynasties, states, and cultures, putting in their places new administrative units and cultural expressions. At first the old systems fought back, but then they gradually accommodated themselves to the new influences and, in turn, had dramatic effects on the conquerors. What characterized this period perhaps more than any other factor was the great movement and mixing of peoples and ideas. This dynamic condition brought with it a profound need for institutions and ideas which could provide stability to the society and the individuals within it.

New groupings and cults rose out of the political and social conditions as people sought fresh divine protectors in both the larger physical world which resulted from Alexander's conquests, and the larger cultural world which brought the unspeculative man face to face with cosmic universals. The conditions and transitoriness of life brought an interest in immortality and a desire to escape from an uncomfortable present. Curiosity about the supernatural and a desire for revelation became the source of the secrets of the universe. Divine protectors were sought as security against the jarring forces of the here and now. Political events changed the world out of all recognition. The settled little worlds in which most had lived were gone, and vast uncertainty replaced them. The once neat little world was now ruled by blind fortune or unchangeable fate.

Judaism was just one of many social forces of this tumultuous world.

54

Its own role was complicated. On the one hand, it had to fight to maintain its hold on the faithful as it was confronted by the unsettling conditions and the attractions of new cultures. On the other hand, its historical drive for converts had operated within narrow limits, and now vast new territories opened as Jews spread throughout the Greco-Roman world. But Judaism also faced challenges in the numerous cults and philosophies of the area and in the state religions which functioned to stabilize the ruling establishment.

The conquerors did not force their beliefs and worship patterns on the conquered. While Jews, and after them Christians and Muslims, expected conquered peoples to take on their faith or pay dearly for the privilege of not doing so, with rare exceptions this was not the attitude of the Greeks and Romans. Their pattern was quite different. They were not exclusivist. They had no dogmas to accept or reject. Moreover, the religions with which they came into contact were not religions in the sense usually understood if Judaism and Christianity are the norms. As a result, the Greeks and Romans tended to regard new expressions of worship as supplements, not substitutes, for what they already had, and they frequently incorporated the deities and rites of conquered peoples, especially when their own system was inferior. This process, which A. D. Nock calls "adhesion," was not the taking on of a new way accompanied by a rejection of the old. Thus it was quite distinct from conversion, which Nock defines as a great change from the old, which is now perceived as wrong, to the new, which is right.[1]

For the classical Greek, religion was approximated by the word *eusebeia,* which means the regular performance of due worship in the proper spirit. The place of faith as it is known in Judaism and Christianity is taken by myth and ritual. There is an implied attitude rather than a conviction. This is why so many in the Greco-Roman world did not become totally converted to Judaism. While there were also other reasons, the chief one was that this simply was not their way. They could adhere to various Jewish practices, such as Sabbath observance, lighting of candles on special occasions, fasting, and abstaining from eating certain foods; but converting to a totally new system was beyond the realm of the possible for most of them. Their systems allowed "adhesion" while Judaism, and later Christianity and Islam, demanded renunciation of the old and starting anew.

Someone within such a system could use Mithraism without belonging to it body and soul. Judaism, however, in effect said to the man who was thinking of becoming a proselyte: you have been a sinner—make a new start; put aside idolatry and the immoral practices which go with it; become a naturalized member of the chosen people; live as God's law commands and you will have every hope of a share in the life of the world to come.[2]

There was nothing like this kind of call among the rivals of Judaism and Christianity. Genuine conversion to paganism came only when Christianity had become so powerful that its rivals became entities by opposition and contrast. It was hard to convert to the cults because there was nothing to seize: there was no theology or hierarchy. The mysteries provided revelation but not dogma. To the ancients the essence of religion was the rite, a process for securing and maintaining correct relations with the world of uncharted forces, and myth, which gave the traditional reason for the rite. None of the mystery cults had an institutional framework of the sort which held and spread Judaism and Christianity.

Unlike the cults, Judaism and Christianity felt that theirs was the only true God. Those worshipping other gods were idolaters and sinners. Though it was not possible for the Jew or Christian, the devotee of Isis could think that his cult was the original and best expression of a devotion voiced by all men in their several ways. Such men saw the synagogue as the center of a philosophical school and could recognize the god of the Jews as a fit object of worship and as capable of equation with a deity of their own, such as Zeus or Dionysus or Attis. New composites were formed as a result of give-and-take on both sides. Thus we find the Jewish god in magic papyri and the practice of Jewish customs, as already noted. But this kind of reciprocity was not possible within the Jewish framework.

Conversion to a philosophy was not unlike conversion to Judaism. The many schools which developed—Pythagoreans, Epicureans, Cynics, and Stoics as well as others—called for something very like conversion. Plato spoke of the object of education as a "turning around of the soul" (*Republic* 7. 518). In a similar vein, Cebes taught that "if a man comes to know, folly disappears and he is saved: he becomes blessed and happy throughout his whole life" (*Pictures*, chap. 3, 1st). As with Judaism and Christianity, philosophy offered life with a scheme, a method to tame passions and enable men to live in accordance with natural law; it provided a sense of unity and produced saints and striking ideal types. It produced dogmatic philosophy for the purpose of saving souls. It was much more successful in winning converts than the mysteries, which, while they evoked strong emotional responses and touched the soul deeply for a moment, did not turn men from evil or hold before them a good toward which they could tend.[3]

Because Rome excelled in conservative administration, its leaders worried much about unwarranted innovations. Included in this concern was religion and the fear that cults could be utilized as mass movements against the state. Public worship therefore became a public concern. Foreign cults were regulated under a special commission. This general practice encouraged conquered peoples to give to their gods Roman names. Shrines were allowed to foreigners in Rome, although from time to time restrictions were placed on them, and there were occasional persecutions. Within this environment, except for occasional and brief periods, Jews and Judaism were tolerated. At times, when proselytizing was prohibited, tensions would grow and the Jews, particularly in Palestine, would rebel against Roman authority and administrative abuse.

Within the multifarious panoply of cults and philosophies, Judaism was sufficiently different to attract special attention by many. Large numbers of Romans were apparently drawn to it. While a number of converts are known to have been made, many more may have been influenced by Judaism to one extent or another. A full conversion, as noted already, was unusual in the Greco-Roman environment and would have meant breaking too many ties. That many gentiles attended Jewish services, however, may be seen from the following contemporary statement by Juvenal: "in which synagogue shall I search thee?" (*Satires* 3. 296, 14; 96–196).[4] It is going too far to say with Josephus that the conquered gave their laws to the conquerors, but the influence was considerable (*Against Apion* 2. 282). It also seems to have been fashionable for aristocratic members of Roman society to adopt some Jewish practices, though these may not have been deeply effective.

The attractions of Judaism seem to have included the following factors: its rationalism in the face of the multiplicity of gods of the cults, all of which seemed limited; the practical realization of a moral and happy life; and the general fashion of patronizing oriental religions.[5] The loyalty of the Jews to the state, their antiquity, admiration for their sacred books and their steadfastness in their own religion, all lent force to Judaism's attractiveness.[6] The heroism of the Jews in challenging Roman imperial power, and their religious loyalty even after defeat, drew many to side with them, even including some of the Roman soldiers who participated in the siege of Jerusalem in 70 c.e.[7] When Flavia, an outstanding Roman noblewoman and the wife of a highly placed senator, converted, Tiberius presented a law to the Senate directing that the Jews of Rome leave immediately on pain of becoming slaves for life unless they gave up Judaism.[8] During this reign, thousands of Jewish youths were sent to Sardinia to fight the brigands of that island and were forced to violate the Sabbath during their training.[9] That a number of Romans did convert is testified to by the graves of proselytes that have been uncovered in the Jewish catacombs in Rome.[10]

As a community the Jews were generally loyal to the state in which they lived. They also served willingly in the army. Because of this, and the recognition of their special religion, they were usually tolerated. Theoretically this toleration was extended only to those born Jewish. Technically, proselytizing was an indictable offense, but the Roman authorities enforced this law only in times of stress.[11] A complicating factor was the feeling that Jews were aloof and felt superior. This led to the dilemma of privileges with persecutions.[12] Although the Jews remained open to converts, this openness was balanced by an exclusiveness which was considered necessary as a barrier to excessive pagan influence. Thus, while society in general was opening, the Jews, to some extent, were closing in. The Jews maintained their peculiar practices, separating themselves socially by not dining with gentiles, because of their dietary regulations, and by shunning the theater, public festivals, and gymnasia. Such exclusivity and obstinate unsociability created resentment and hatred, but as supporters of the regimes they gained the protection of kings and emperors, also a factor in further alienating the Jews from the general population.[13]

A somewhat varying view holds that the Jewish drive for cultural and religious survival was balanced by a greater openness toward gentiles than at any other time in Jewish history. While the Jews might have remained aloof from gentiles, living securely with the special privileges which were necessary for their life style, they were such enthusiastic missionaries that they destroyed their security. Missionary activity brought about their expulsion from Rome in 139 b.c.e. and again by

Tiberius (14–37 c.e.) and Claudius (41–57). Even during the wars of the first century the Flavians had to take measures to make the circumcision of gentiles a capital offense.[14]

There was considerable anti-Jewish feeling in the Roman Empire. It apparently was not racist, but was based on political, social, and religious factors. There was a feeling that the Jews felt themselves to be superior.[15] While the Romans, controlling the empire, felt no physical threat from the Jews in these areas, Greeks and others, particularly in Asia Minor, felt themselves threatened politically and economically. This was also true in Mesopotamia, Palestine, and Egypt, where the Jews were tolerated, protected, and given special privileges by the Romans. At times, also, the Jews sought to gain citizenship in cities, which was denied them unless they converted to Greek culture and cults.[16]

On occasion this mass resentment of the Jews was shared by local Roman officials. In the first century in Egypt this resentment was expressed violently. To an old literary tradition of anti-Jewish feeling was added a political cause. With the Roman takeover the Greeks lost many of their rights, while those of the Jews were confirmed. Further, they governed themselves through an ethnarch. The anger of the Greeks was vented on the Jews, whom they identified with Rome and saw as favorites of their oppressors.[17] Violence broke into the open about 38 c.e., when the mad Caligula reigned and Rome was weak.[18]

Anti-Jewish sentiment was also fanned in Rome by the Stoics, who aspired to establish a religious philosophy for the general populace and pursued a course of vigorous missionary propaganda. They saw the Jews, especially in the East, as not only obstinate opponents but dangerous rivals. They became the first professional Jew-haters.[19]

Jews and Judaism were generally tolerated and protected by Rome. Most Roman legislation was not so much anti-Jewish but had as its purpose the isolating of Judaism to keep it from spreading and possibly undermining the Roman system.[20] Rome was not afraid of hypothetical messianic armies in the future, but of actual or possible Jewish rebellions, which proved difficult to suppress. Tacitus expressed this concern when he characterized proselytes as *transgressi in morem eorum* and as renegades of the fatherland, *exuere patriam* (*Hist.* 5. 5.).[21] Specific legislation to prevent such proselytizing, which also served to remove citizens from the imperial cult, took several forms through the years. Vespasian (69–79 c.e.) instituted a tax on the Jews for the temple of Jupiter Capitolinus in Rome, which may have discouraged some prospective prose-lytes. Domitian (81–96) was more effective, for he hunted out proselytes, encouraged denunciation of them, and sentenced Jews to death for atheism if they persisted in converting. Nerva (96–98) removed the privileges given to *delatores* (informers) but exacted no punishment for the denial of the imperial cult. The Hadrianic persecutions following the failure of the Bar Kochba revolt, which prohibited circumcision and the accepting of converts, made that period difficult. Antoninus Pius (138–61) forbade circumcision to those not born Jewish. Septimus Severus (193–211) forbade proselytizing and conversion. Yet, with the exception of Hadrian (117–38), none of the emperors acted against Judaism or the privileges attached to it. They only sought to prevent its spreading. The consistency of this legislation testifies to the continued Jewish practice of proselytizing.[22]

10

The Rise of Christianity and Its Effects

In its earliest stages Christianity was neither a threat to Judaism nor was it considered as very different from it. Jesus saw his mission as one to his fellow Jews exclusively. He came, as he said, not to destroy but to fulfill. "Not one jot or tittle was to pass from the law." The two great commandments elicited from him by the Pharisees were both from the Old Testament: thou shalt love the Lord thy God, and thou shalt love thy neighbor as thyself. During the early stages of its development, Rome viewed Christianity as a subdivision of Judaism. Only after a general failure to convert their fellow Jews and a series of other events did Christians, under the leadership of Paul and others, move to convert gentiles. Gradually it became apparent that Christianity was a movement separate from Judaism. It then became the object of special concern, discrimination, and persecution by the authorities.

In time Christians came to seem as dangerous in Roman eyes as heretics were in medieval Europe. The Romans were fearful of sedition stirred up under the guise of religion. Of particular concern was the Christian teaching of the kingdom of God. Indicative of this is the statement of Justin Martyr: "You, having heard that we expect a kingdom, have formed the uncritical impression that we mean a kingdom in the human sense" (1. 2). After the Bar Kochba revolt in 135, such themes were bound to arouse suspicion. While it seemed queer that Jews would not worship the emperor, it was considered dangerous that Christians did not. One reason for this is that the Jews were perceived as a religious nationality, termed a *natio* before 70 and a *religio licita* after that.[1] Christianity, on the other hand, had never had a state and so, by definition, it was guilty of apostasy from the state, or atheism—that is, not

61

worshipping the deities of the state. It was this combination of religion and politics which brought about the Christian difficulty.[2] The welfare of the Roman state was seen as dependent upon the performance of the traditional Roman rites. Christianity, with its drive for converts and its theology, was felt to be a threat to the Roman religious system.

Gradually Christianity became not a threat, but the force used to keep the empire unified. Rather than oppose it, the emperors, beginning with Constantine (327–37), adopted Christianity to save the empire. Christianity's organization, which developed its theology and moral dogma, and administered its works of charity and benevolence, could possibly bring the crumbling empire together into a new commonality. Large numbers of people came into the faith, now no longer a small new branch of Judaism. Nock writes that the success of the Christian mission in winning converts rested on the central idea of divinity brought into humanity, together with the promise of salvation.[3] Further: "The success of Christianity is the success of an institution which united the sacramentalism and the philosophy of the time. It satisfied the in-quiring turn of mind, the desire for escape from fate, the desire for security in the hereafter; like Stoicism, it gave a way of life and made man at home in the universe, but unlike Stoicism it did for the ignorant as well as for the lettered. It satisfied also social needs and it secured men against loneliness."[4] In addition, many Christian theological ideas were not alien to most of the populace. They already knew that a god could have a son. Trinities were not new. Life, like myth, was known to have its allegorical meaning.[5] The son of a god could die, although it was peculiar that he would suffer and die voluntarily. It was proper that a god not be addressed directly but that "the Father be approached through the son."[6] The idea of community support and immediate mem-bership and welcome in churches wherever Christians lived, and the doctrine of last things, were new for gentiles but old in Judaism. "The Christian householder brought forth from his store things old and new: the old was not obsolete and the new was not incomprehensible."[7] The only serious challenge to Christianity came from Manichaeism. The latter was defeated, not only because it arose after Christianity was al-ready fairly well established, but because it offered a standard of per-fection which was for the few.

Christianity served Rome as Judaism could not. Judaism remained tied to the idea of its own unique role and mission, standing aside from total commitment to any state. National aspirations were never totally absent. While Judaism accepted and even zealously sought converts, conversion to Judaism entailed more of a total cultural as well as religious commitment than did conversion to Christianity. Apologetics on loyalty to the empire and prayers for the emperor appear early in Christian literature. The Jews, however, felt that they had to survive as a special group to keep alive the idea of God which all mankind would eventually follow. While the Jews could live as citizens or as tolerated populace in any state, they continued to envisage the time when all mankind would join their polity. Because of this "national-political" content, Judaism could not be accepted as a universal religion: its aim was to "Israelize" the world, to impose its religious truths and customs and social practices, and those who joined it would have to denationalize themselves and become incorporated into the Jewish nation.[8] Christianity was far more accommodating in its demands and could be used easily by a political power.[9]

Once Christianity was enrolled in the service of the state, the state began to serve the church in a way which further enhanced the unity of the state. Prohibitions were early placed on Judaism, the religion out of which Christianity came. The very missionary zeal which Christianity learned from mother Judaism, and which led to its growth, was made illegal for Jews. The faith that invented such themes as conversion and missions now found its opportunity to practice them severely limited wherever Christianity dominated, and even further limited within a few centuries with the rise of Islam.

The first "Christian" emperor prohibited Jews from receiving converts. In 339 C.E. marriages between Jews and Christians were prohibited. Somewhat later, slaves could not be converted without their being forfeited. The third and fourth councils of Orleans, 538–45, decreed that Christians could not take part in Jewish banquets, and again Jews were not allowed to take proselytes. Everything was done to keep Jews from influencing Christians and possible converts to Christianity. In 357, apostasy from Christianity was declared a crime punishable by property confiscation, and Jews who encouraged a return to Judaism suffered the same penalty. Laws promulgated in 409 and 438 established capital punishment for the proselyting Jew. Thus, the persecuted religion became the persecutor. An omen of still more extreme measures to come is seen in the language of the laws, which is vulgar and abusive. Judaism is called a nefarious sect and the synagogue *a concilium dearum,* slang for "brothel." [10]

Doubtless the church felt itself threatened by Judaism, both as the source of Christianity and as a competitor for converts. Thus, the first law of the empire in which the influence of the church could be traced (315) was the prohibition of Jewish missionary activity and the death penalty for the convert to the *nefaria secta.* The amazing thing at this time and in the centuries which followed—indeed, until the disappearance of the Inquisition in the nineteenth century—is that Jews continued in any conversionist activity at all. The fact that they did get converts in both Christian and Islamic lands is indicative of the authenticity and importance of conversionist activity within Judaism.

Under Christianity Jews did continue to seek converts where they could, and even where it was prohibited. But, as will be seen, such instances would of necessity occur on a far more limited basis. Christianity now saw itself as the fulfilled Judaism, with the obligation of converting mankind to the one true faith. As convinced as Judaism was, Christianity went even further with its declaration of *nulla salus extra ecclesiam,* "no salvation is possible outside of Christianity."

Just as Judaism gradually developed its role as a universal faith with the mission of bringing others to the worship of the one true God through the process of conversion, so did Christianity and later Islam. It is not correct that "Christianity and Islam were from the start universal and world-conquering faiths, in which missionary work was a central and essential element." [11] As noted above, Christianity began with its message directed exclusively to Jews. More will be detailed of Islam, which began with a narrow program for the Arabic tribes of northwest Arabia and only gradually broadened its scope as a conquering missionary faith. Judaism was the model for both of them in most respects, although since the pattern had already been established, they developed more rapidly and more broadly.

PART III

THE MEDIEVAL PERIOD:
From the Rise of Islam to
the French Revolution

11
Historical Overview

THE MILLENNIUM and more following the establishment of Christianity as the religion of the Roman Empire, and the rise and success of Islam, was a period when Jews were generally embattled. Virtually all Jews lived under either Christian or Muslim domination. In Christian lands the Jews were confronted by two attitudes, neither of which was very salutory: at times they were hounded, it seems, almost to physical extinction; on other occasions, it was decreed that they survive in order that they might acknowledge the truth of Christianity and convert. It was considered an affront to Christianity that the people from whom Jesus had come persistently refused to accept him. Somehow the validity of the Christian's own religion was thus jeopardized. Where the Jews were allowed to live, their lives were made harsh.

Special persecutions arising out of specific problems were constant during this period. Mass expulsions began with that from England in 1290, followed by others from France, parts of Germany, and finally, and most dramatically, from Spain in 1492 and ten years later from Portugal. Restrictions and discrimination were part of both the legal and social systems of Christian Europe. The pressures of this society gradually forced the Jewish community in upon itself. It became increasingly more introspective and isolated. Its concern with the outside world was replaced by the drive to survive. All of its adaptive energies were directed toward this end. While ideologically it was still concerned with bringing all men to the one God, in practice this goal would have to await another day, perhaps even the messianic age. Converts were still made but apparently in smaller numbers, and frequently without encouragement on the part of Jews. Even in the centuries following the French Revolution, when the hold of medievalism was virtually broken, Jewish militancy for converts was not restored. For too

67

long had the Jews followed another course, and even more time would be required to renew old patterns, if they were to be renewed at all.

Christianity became a world faith through a series of unpredictable circumstances. From a small group of Jews seeking to reform their own faith grew a religion which spread first throughout the Mediterranean world and then, as a part of European culture, to the rest of the world as the imperial powers made conquests on every continent. Similarly, in the seventh century, Mohammed, an orphan in the city of Mecca in northwestern Arabia, developed a religion for a limited community. It became one of the forces leading to a great Arabic-Islamic empire which stretched from Spain to India within one hundred years.

Mohammed's plan had been to raise the moral level of his people, care for the social needs of a changing society, and unify warring tribes.[1] The models for his faith were Judaism and, to a lesser extent, Christianity. He was guided by the Bible and other Jewish sources. To a limited extent he unified parts of Arabia. After his death, his friends and disciples collected certain of his sayings into the Koran. Using this as the basis of their organization and inspiration, Arabic tribes spilled out of the Arabian peninsula to spread their faith as they conquered. Coming into the areas occupied by the Persian and Roman Empires, which had sorely weakened themselves through long conflict with each other, the Arabs, to their own surprise, conquered quickly and broadly. Opposition was slight from the old imperial forces, and the local populations, more often than not, welcomed the new conquerors, who they hoped would be an improvement on their former rulers.

In this way the vast majority of Jews, living in West Asia, North Africa and Spain, came under Muslim rule. The immediate effect for them was improvement. They ceased to be an outcast community persecuted by the ruling church and became a part of the vast class of Muslim subjects with special status. According to Mohammed's teachings, monotheists were to be tolerated as "people of the book." Jews and Christians were not to have the same status as Muslims, but force was not to be used against them to alter their religion. Generally, the subject peoples were less oppressed than under Byzantium. For the most part the Jews welcomed the Muslims and were regarded by them as allies. This was particularly true during the conquest of Spain.

Yet within Islam there were seeds of anti-Jewish sentiment. In Medina, Mohammed's first seat of power, the Jews were numerous and prominent. Once Mohammed was established there, he expected the Jews to join him and his new religion. When they would not, they earned the prophet's enmity. There is a deep ambivalence toward the Jews in the Koran. Biblical prophets are exalted and Jew and Arab are seen to have the same progenitor in Abraham. Yet the Jews rejected the new prophet who was the "seal of the prophets." Proximity may also have bred a certain amount of contempt. Some historians believe that Mohammed required Jewish tribal lands as a reward for his followers, and so rationalized taking them from the Jews.[2] Yet, while Christianity gradually disappeared in various parts of the Muslim Empire, the Jewish community survived.

Tolerance toward non-Muslims lessened in the second and especially the third century of the Muslim era, about 900. Many humiliating restrictions were placed on Jews and Christians. They were forced to dress differently, could not hold certain government posts, could not build new houses of worship or ride on certain animals. Gradually the legal structure of Islam was elaborated, and as Islam spread among the conquered peoples, it became more restrictive. Frequently these laws were not enforced, but during periods of duress they were available. The particular conditions of the Jews varied with the regime after the central control of the Arabic Empire broke down in the eighth century. For instance, under the Fatimids in Egypt (969–1171), Jews fared very well, with the exception of a violent outbreak against them at the end of the tenth century. The Berber dynasty of Morocco, the Almohades, was very repressive, destroying old Jewish communities and forcing conversion even though this was against Islamic law. Conversion to Judaism was apparently rare in Islamic lands. The Jewish communities, as in Christian countries, abandoned their conversionist mission and became enclaves bent on insuring the survival of those who were born into the faith.

New ideas and ways of organizing society gradually developed in Europe during the Renaissance. Religion was replaced by nationalism as the major method of organizing people. Uniformity of religion, which had been the major device for bringing masses of people together, was supplanted by a sense of having a similar history, language, and culture as the basis of the state. Citizenship was broadened to include peoples of diverse religions or no religion at all. Loyalty to the state rather than to a faith became the crucial factor. In such places, particularly in

America and in parts of Europe, the condition of the Jew improved in many ways.

Though he did not often take advantage of the situation, the Jew was now as free as the Christian to seek converts. Of course, now that religion had become less vital than before, the drive for converts had relaxed in all religions. In Muslim lands, these changes came much later and are still in the process of development. But they will not affect Jews in any event, since virtually no Jews now live in Muslim lands.

12
Christianity and Conversion to Judaism

THE ATTITUDE of Christianity toward conversion to Judaism may be easily and concisely summarized: it was prohibited. While Jews and Judaism might be tolerated, this was only that Jews might convert to Christianity in fulfillment of the Old Testament prophecy. That Judaism, however, still appeared attractive to many gentiles, including Christians, is obvious from the repeated prohibitions of conversion to Judaism, which entailed dramatic punishments for anyone involved. A motivation other than merely preventing conversion to Judaism seems to have been behind the laws and propaganda, particularly in the twelfth and thirteenth centuries, when the church's power and expansion were at their peak. The spread of Albigensian and other heretical movements may have lent some validity to the never-ending suspicion that professing Jews helped stimulate Christian heterodoxies. But the taint of Jewish influence was in all probability also used to stigmatize any religious opponent of the church, such as a Jew or a carrier of Jewish influences. The occasional conversions of Christians, including clergy, reinforced this fear, and it was used as a device against dissidence within the church structure.[1]

In Christian circles it became common to accuse opponents of "Judaizing." For the most part, Jews had no direct role in the development and promotion of the heresies and other movements that were charged with Judaizing. Occasionally an individual Jewish scholar may have been consulted, or a Jewish book used to bolster a belief, but the heresies grew out of social forces in the communities which spawned them. The first use of this kind of accusation seems to have been at the Council of Laodicea in the fourth century, when Christian ecclesiastics such as Agobard charged other Christians at Lyons with Jewish inclinations and

71

habits. Roman Catholics used the same charge to disparage the movements of Wycliffe and Lollard, and against Reuchlin, Luther, Melanchthon, Zwingli, Calvin, and their contemporaries. The Reformers, in turn, made the same accusations against their opponents. Thus did Calvin accuse Servetius and Luther, Muenster, and other Hebraists of the day. During their ascendancy, accusations of Judaizing were the favorite mode of attack on Puritans by both Papists and Protestant adversaries. In terms of direct influence by Jews, such accusations were meaningless.[2]

Preventing conversion to Judaism was accomplished by separating Jews from Christians and making the act of conversion a costly one. Early, after the establishment of a formal relationship between Christianity and the empire, decrees making conversion illegal were promulgated. Other laws forbade the selling of slaves to Jews. Christian virgins and widows were not allowed to marry Jews. Under Gratian (359–83), anyone who converted was deprived of testamentary rights, with the same penalty applied to the Jew who received him. Theodosius the Great (379–95) made marriage to a Jew or Jewess equivalent to adultery. In Spain the era of persecutions was opened by King Sisebut in 612. This Visigoth decreed that no Christian might be in a position dependent on a Jew. Jews were required to give up their Christian servants, slaves, and tenants. Lands held in lease were to be transferred to Christians, and slaves were set free. A Jew who converted a Christian to Judaism was to suffer death and confiscation of his property. Children conceived of Christian female slaves by Jewish masters were to be reared as Christians. Jews were encouraged to convert. These laws shook the foundations of Jewish economic life. Jews could no longer cultivate or even own large estates. A short time later Sisebut ordered the Jews to either convert or leave the country.[3] In 1233 Pope Gregory IX, in a letter, admonished the clergy of Germany regarding Christians who "of their own free will, adopt their [the Jews'] faith, following their rites, and permit themselves to be circumcised, publically professing themselves Jews."[4] Similar accusations were frequently echoed in the twelfth and thirteenth centuries by both ecclesiastical and secular authorities. Various laws were either restated or introduced to cope with what was a continuing problem.

Several instances of punishment for involvement in conversion are recorded. One involves the deacon of Oxford, who converted and married a Jewess. He was condemned and publicly burned in 1222. On the strength of a rumor that they were converting Christians, the Jews of Majorca were sentenced in 1315 to have all their property confiscated and to be deprived of their privileges. The sentence was annulled after the pledging of so large an amount to the king that the community was in debt for several years.[5] In 1278 Rabbi Isaac Males of Toulouse was burned by the Inquisition on the charge of proselyting.[6]

Religious law provided the means for limiting the influence and power which Jews might achieve, particularly as their numbers in Europe increased. The Jews were to be clearly marked with special clothing and emblems. Economic opportunities were circumscribed in scope. These laws, greatly broadened, were formalized by the Third Lateran Council (1179), led by Innocent III. While the result of these laws was to narrow the range of Jewish enterprise, preserving advantage for Christians, any proselyting in which Jews might wish to engage was also affected.

13

The Jewish Adaptation to Restrictions on Conversion

IN SPITE of the pressures of the Christian church and society, some conversion to Judaism took place in medieval times. Estimates of its extent vary, as will be seen below. Increasingly, however, Jewish law and attitudes began to alter in response to the general hostility to Judaism. There remains some controversy concerning the pace and nature of the changes. Maimonides' teaching that Christians and Muslims were monotheists, and therefore need not convert to worship God, may be seen as limiting the drive to seek proselytes. On the other hand, seeing Judaism as containing a spiritual aristocracy, Maimonides would have the sincere convert fully accepted after severe screening.

A somewhat different approach which may also involve acceptance of the limits on conversion is that of Judah HaLevi. As compensation for the harshness of the Jewish condition, he revived the idea of the Jews as the chosen people, physically as well as spiritually. The superiority of the Jews was such that a proselyte, while he might be pious, could not receive the gift of prophecy, which was reserved for born Jews. The intrinsic nature of the Jew was special, and this specialness could not be acquired by an act of will. The convert could grow nearer to God but could not reach the highest level of religious attainment, prophecy. As if in answer to such an approach, the *Zohar* states that when a proselyte becomes a Jew, a new soul descends on him from heaven, yet this soul is not quite of the same high spiritual caliber as the souls of born Jews.

Jacob Katz holds that it was in the mutual interest of both Christians and Jews, in the period from the tenth to the fourteenth century, to adopt patterns of segregation. The religious demands of each faith, as

74

well as the danger of reciprocal influence of one on the other, brought about the maintenance of a rigid standard of mutual exclusiveness. At the same time both faiths left themselves open to being joined by outsiders. The possibility of all Christians converting to Judaism was more remote than the opposite, so the defensiveness of the Jewish communities was well founded. The conversion of whole communities of Jews under dire threat was not uncommon even though many of those converted might revert to Judaism.[1]

With all of the pressures on them, medieval Jewry remained convinced of Judaism's truth, its superiority, and its religious mission. Yet sentiment did begin to change. The strongest position against proselytizing was taken by Rabbi Simon Luria in the mid-sixteenth century. In commenting on the law that a proselyte would have to be accepted if he persisted, even after being warned of his obligations and of the dangers, Luria stated that this law referred to a different place and radically different conditions. He felt that the Jews were not living in their own land, and conversion would seriously endanger the Jewish community. His views may have been motivated by the accusation, about 1539, that the Jews of Cracow and other neighboring towns had persuaded Christians to become Jews, sending them to Turkey after they were circumcised to remove evidence of guilt. Luria might also have feared that the protection of the Jewish community would be withdrawn should conversion to Judaism be encouraged. The threat to the Jews was too great, and proselytizing would endanger their survival.[2]

Just how effective this attitude was may be seen from the history of the Spanish-Portuguese Jewish community in England following its restoration in the mid-seventeenth century. After having been absent from England for more than 350 years following the expulsion in 1290, the first established Jewish community—a few individuals had been there earlier—was highly defensive, and this attitude lasted for more than 200 years. At the time of the founding of the community in 1657 there were as many as four converts in the congregation.[3] However, the leaders of the Jewish community assumed that one of the conditions of the readmission was that they not seek to convert, or unduly influence, Christians. For this reason the Jewish community enacted a number of anti-proselytizing laws. In effect in 1664 was a prohibition against any argument on a religious subject with non-Jews and any attempts at proselytizing. In 1671 even the temporary employment of Christian maids was prohibited, since they might convert. It is possible that the Jews were concerned because of the increased anti-Catholic agitation at the time, since the English tended to bracket all foreigners with Catholics. A law of 1678 specified that anyone who harbored a convert even for one night would be treated as seriously as one who made a convert. Proselytes entering Judaism after 1660 were not permitted to pray in the synagogue, and in 1681 it was ruled that anyone who was present at a conversion would be fined ten pounds and excommunicated. In 1751 it was specified that even those converted by foreign Jews were not acceptable, and anyone who aided in such a process—for instance by sending someone to Holland for conversion—would be expelled from the community and not allowed burial in the Jewish burial grounds. Well into the nineteenth century proselytes could still not be made in the Sephardic community although some were accepted by the Ashkenazim. The first conversion in the history of the Sephardic community took place in 1877 with Rabbi Artom officiating. His successor, Moses Gaster, followed this precedent with permission of the council when he became rabbi in 1887.[4]

The situation in England was complicated by the general dynastic difficulties, the reign of Oliver Cromwell, and the rise of militant and extreme Puritans, many of whom favored Jewish practices and even affiliated with Jewish congregations on the continent. In 1624 one James Whitehall was imprisoned for preaching Judaism at Christ Church in Oxford. Mary Chester was persecuted for "Judaical" practices in 1635. John Traske gained a number of followers for his version of Puritanism, which was close to Orthodox Judaism in its Sabbath and food practices. After appearing before the court of Star Chamber, he was branded with a *J* on his forehead and imprisoned. He finally recanted though his wife did not. One of his cohorts, Hamlet Jackson, went to Amsterdam, where he was circumcised; together with some others, he converted and lived as a Noachite. This was in the early seventeenth century. These and similar events, though not directly initiated by Jews, explain the Jewish community's sensitivity in regard to conversion. So strong was this concern that it continued well into the nineteenth century.[5]

Ben Zion Wachholder, in a number of articles, disagrees with the conventional scholarly view that medieval rabbis generally discouraged proselytizing. Using the responsa and Halachah of the tosafists as his main source, Wachholder concludes that the church was not motivated solely by politics in its condemnation of conversion to Judaism, using fear of proselytizing as a blind. Rather, he says, conversion to Judaism took place with considerable frequency and thus was seen as a threat by the church. Wachholder deals with twenty-one responsa which are concerned with the problems of twenty-five converts in the twelfth, thirteenth, and fourteenth centuries.[6]

In one instance a Jewish woman had a gentile lover. Her husband divorced her and she became a Christian. When she later reverted to Judaism, her gentile husband converted and they were married as Jews. Their adulterous relationship was discounted. Another responsum indicates that during the latter half of the twelfth century a family of proselytes flourished in northern France, apparently unmolested by both the church and the local authorities.[7] Both canon and secular laws prohibiting proselytes were ignored in this instance and in five similar cases involving the inheritance of proselytes' property.[8]

That this was a period of ardent church action against proselytizing indicates that such laws were not universally enforced. For in addition to the cases noted above, during the thirteenth century the Inquisition burned proselytes at the stake in England, France, and Germany. A case is also recorded of a convert not being circumcised out of fear of the local authorities.[9] Rabbi Meir of Rothenburg (d. 1293) tells of a proselyte who was detected by local authorities through the negligence of some Jews. He was redeemed for thirty coins.[10] As conditions became more difficult, the fact of a person's conversion was omitted from such documents as marriage contracts and divorce certificates.

That the rabbis did not discourage converts may also be seen in the fact that many of the converts lived in the homes of tosafists and became rabbinic students. Some were known as scholars. Wachholder does not find the slightest hint of discouragement or unfriendliness toward proselytes on the part of Jews. The statement of Rabbi Gershon ben Jacob Ha-Gozer, that a candidate for conversion be rejected three times because he might be a cause of danger, is seen as an isolated utterance and is not repeated in any code or comment of the other tosafists. If a convert indicates fear of being found out, says Rabbi Jacob ben Moses Moelln (Maharil), writing in the fifteenth century, it is permissible to reject him and to inform the authorities if he persists. Generally, the fourteenth- and fifteenth-century codes continued to produce laws on proselytes as if the Inquisition did not exist. Most of the converts seem to have belonged to the upper and middle classes, although this may only appear to be so because those with substantial material possessions were likely subjects for the responsa literature. There does not, however, appear to be evidence of popular enthusiasm for conversion among the Christian masses, nor of a formal mission by Jews.

Rabbi Shimon ben Zemach Duran (Rashbaz, 1361–1444) argued that seeking proselytes should be considered as one of the 613 biblical commandments. Others, including Maimonides and Nachmanides, disagreed. This is seen by Wachholder as indicative of the more restrictive attitude of the scholars of Spain compared with those in France and Germany. Yet if proselytizing is a commandment, then it is of more than theoretical interest and so must be continued, despite prohibitions. If it was only a voluntary act, then external laws might be binding. The fact that during the Middle Ages Jews jeopardized their lives and property by accepting proselytes is indicative of the fact that they regarded proselytizing as a commandment.[11] However, the *Shulhan Arukh* (1567) codified the more rigorous Halachah in line with the Spanish school, though allowing for the acceptance of some converts. Gradually the Spanish school prevailed, preventing a more positive attitude toward proselytizing.

14
Conversions During
the Middle Ages

GIVEN the general situation, one might anticipate that only a small number of conversions would have taken place during the Middle Ages. However, the sources reveal a considerable group of converts, primarily from the clergy and upper classes.[1] It is to be expected, because of the dangers involved, that few of the conversions in this period would be recorded, but even in freer societies exact records are rarely kept. Various estimates have been suggested. According to one, Middle Eastern and North African Jewry doubled between the seventh and eighth centuries as a result of the proselyting of slaves.[2] The slave markets during this period were glutted by captives taken during the Muslim conquests. In the region of Pferse in Germany, based on memorial book information, hundreds are estimated to have become Jews.[3] Baron estimates that the Jewish population of Europe grew from 850,000 in 1660 to 12,500,000 in 1940, a rise of 1500 percent, as contrasted with increases of 250 percent in the world population and 350 percent in the European population during the same period.[4] Such a dramatic increase can be accounted for by better hygienic practices and large-scale conversions. Isolated references such as the following indicate that many references to Jewish conversionary efforts and activities may have been lost. For example, Antoine Biet, a French priest traveling in Martinique in 1654, wrote that the Jews "were permitted in the Island to Judaize, and in the sight of all the world to exercise their religion and observe their Sabbath."[5]

Slaves provided, perhaps, the largest source of converts during this period. Converting slaves was supported by Jewish law. During the second half of the first millennium, there occurred the greatest religious expansion ever known as Christianity and Islam conquered Europe, North Africa, and Asia Minor. Judaism gained relatively little excepting through the conversion of slaves. As discussed earlier, the practice of integrating slaves into the Jewish group and Judaism had a long history, extending back to the biblical period. The Talmud makes it clear that a slave was to be circumcised and immersed when acquired (*Yevamot* 48b). He was then legally known as an *eved Kena'ani,* a Judaized slave with the obligation of following the same laws that were observed by Jewish women (*Hagigah* 4a, *Nazir* 61a, *Keritot* 7b). Slaves were not allowed to study Torah, wear phylacteries, or constitute one of the quorum required for public worship (*Ketubot* 28, *Gittin* 38a). The talmudic literature sometimes refers to the acquisition of slaves as a holy work since more people are thereby brought to recognize God (*Yer. Avodah Zarah* 1:1). Selling a slave to a gentile, thereby depriving him of the opportunity to worship God, was penalized with a fine of ten times the value of the slave (*Gittin* 4a). When a Jewish slave was manumitted, he was given a certificate, immersed again, and so became a full proselyte.

The quantity of slaves increased greatly in the Geonic period.[6] Manumitting was easier, and many more cases are cited in the literature. Trading in slaves also increased. Nahshon Gaon liberalized the rules governing the trade in non-Jewish slaves. They could be sold if not circumcised. This was probably the result of compelling economic and social factors. At the same time slaves were encouraged to convert and become closer to their Jewish masters within a hostile environment. Conversion was also considered necessary for them to handle food and wine without contaminating them.[7]

The geonim of Sura rejected the idea that freedom of choice played a part in a slave's acceptance of Judaism and refused to consider forced conversion as eternally binding. This was done to facilitate trading and to legitimize children which Jews had by their slaves. Wachholder relates their view to Sura being pragmatic because of its importance as a commercial and political center.[8]

Although there was some decline in the number of responsa regarding slavery in the ninth and tenth centuries, it was dramatic by the eleventh. The Babylonian centers were declining and there was a movement of Jews to Europe, where the feudal system removed the economic substructure for slaves. Also, Christian and Muslim restrictions on owning and converting slaves increased. In the West, under Islam, conversion of slaves was practiced, often in opposition to Islamic law. Because conversion of Muslims and Christians was against the law, instances were seldom recorded. The conversion of a Christian to Judaism is, however, recorded in 1159.[9] The woman who was converted denounced her master before a Muslim judge but then contended that she was the daughter of a Jewess. In Fatimid and Ayyubid times, when some latitude toward conversion was general, the Islamic law against conversion to any faith but Islam was largely disregarded. It seems that many female and male slaves must have been converted to Judaism. Many Jewish freedmen and women are also mentioned in the Geniza records. At the same time, the Jewish authorities do not seem to have insisted that slaves accept baptism.[10]

An Englishman visiting North Africa in the 1670s wrote as follows: "I confess Barbary affords but few of these proselytes: for although there are frequent examples both of Jews and Christians turning Moors, yet very seldom are any met with who turn Jews; which made me less inquisitive after the present manner of receiving Proselytes." [11] He further noted that circumcision was not always followed "for fear that pain and shame would deter."

The converts most frequently mentioned by name in the literature are clergy. Perhaps this is because they were the most notorious. In 839 Bodo, a prominent cleric, embraced Judaism, took the name Eleazar, and married a Jewish girl. He fled to Muslim Spain, a refuge for converts, where he became an active proselytizer.[12] Vecelin converted in late 1012 (some sources have 1005 or 1006).[13] Suspicion of romantic attachments is alleged with the conversion of two Cistercian monks before 1200, and with the already-mentioned deacon of Oxford in 1222.[14] The deacon of Oxford may have come to Judaism through his study of Hebrew. The same is true of a Dominican friar, Robert of Redding, who is said to have been motivated by the study of Hebrew literature. He embraced Judaism, assumed the name Haggai, and took a Jewish wife.[15]

The best-known clerical convert was Obadiah, who was born in Oppido in southern Italy in the third quarter of the eleventh century. Obadiah mentions another convert, Andreas, the archbishop of Bari, who went to Constantinople for his circumcision, then fled to Egypt, where he died in 1078. Obadiah gives Andreas' example as one of the reasons for his own conversion, along with a mystical dream during which he had his first seminal emission. Another priest converted and wrote fourteen pamphlets in an effort to convince his colleagues to do the same. He failed in this attempt, was jailed, and subsequently escaped.[16]

A former monk, Abraham ben Abraham of Wuerzburg, converted, apparently, as a result of using the Vulgate as a crib in his·Pentateuch studies and seeing the unreliability of the translation.[17] Another German, Abraham ben Jacob, illustrated the Amsterdam Haggadah in 1695.[18] That the Jews were not shy in their proselyting may be seen in Abraham Abulafia's attempt to convert Pope Martin IV! Among the seven men and three women proselyte martyrs listed in the memorial book of Mayence (1264–1341) was a French superior of the barefooted friars.[19]

A number of converts from the upper class are also recorded. Political utopian yearnings based on biblical stories seem to have been behind the conversion of Count Raymond of Sens, who proclaimed himself the Jewish king. He is reported to have provoked an attack on Sens by King Robert the Pious, and contributed at least indirectly to the anti-Jewish reaction on the part of the king, which placed all of French Jewry in jeopardy.[20]

A nobleman living near Lyons, about 1575, became convinced of the superiority of Judaism and went to Venice with his two sons and converted.[21] There was also a great number of cases where Christians with Jewish backgrounds were reared as Marranos and eventually reverted to Júdaism. Other random instances of conversion are included here. A congregation of twenty-two proselytes lived in London undisturbed until the pogroms of 1189 exterminated them together with other Jews.[22] Even with the negative attitude of the Spanish rabbis toward proselyting, it appears from a responsum of Rabbi Asher of Castile that converts were still accepted in the 1320s. A rumor that two Germans had been circumcised in Toledo was sufficient to jeopardize the entire Jewish community. These men had come to Spain with the intention of converting and found encouragement and shelter with the Jews of Aragon.[23]

There is also the case of the impoverished widow of a wealthy and prominent man, who went to Narbonne with her three children and there converted to Judaism. Rabbi David, a member of the family of Rabbi Todros of Narbonne, married her. Six months later, learning that her family was seeking her, they moved. Shortly thereafter Rabbi David was killed and two of the three children taken captive. She left with the third, in abject poverty. A fragment of an appeal in her behalf survives.[24]

In 1539 Polish public opinion forced the burning of Malcher, the converted wife of an alderman of Cracow.[25] In the same country the conversion of Count Potacki led to his execution. From Amsterdam, in 1625, there is the burial notice of the wife and children of an English proselyte who had translated the Jewish liturgy into English for her.[26] In 1628 the conversion of Johann Peter Spaeth, who took the name Moses Germanus, caused great furor among orthodox Protestants.[27] A plate in Leon de Modena's *The Rites and Ceremonies of the Jews,* published in London in 1733, has a representation of the Seder meal showing a Negro at the table with the family, indicating that Negro slaves of Amsterdam Jews were converted.[28] In the small community of Sverovoch, near the border of Poland, Lithuania, and Russia, a Jew, Baruch Leibov, built a synagogue across the street from a church and influenced a retired naval captain, Alexander Voznitsin, to study the Bible and finally to convert to Judaism. The public outcry led to their being brought to St. Petersburg and condemned to death. They were burned in the public square on July 15, 1738, warning the Jews against accepting other converts.[29]

15

Socio-Economic
Implications for Conversion

THE JEWS had known several centuries of adjustment experience as a minority-enclave people. Because various groups of Jews lived among different peoples under highly diverse conditions, their adaptations varied. In every instance, however, social and economic differences affected the Jewish attitude toward conversion and the acceptance of converts.

The earliest experience which the Jews had in this regard followed the exile to Babylonia in 586 B.C.E. Their survival pattern rested on stressing specialness in both religion and role. They were to keep themselves holy, witnessing to God's existence and uniqueness that they might bring all men eventually to acknowledge Him and live in accordance with His will. While there were universalist elements in this teaching, its purpose was particularist—the survival of the Jewish people. Gradually a theology and set of rites developed which served to maintain the identity of this people without a land of their own. They became a ritually segregated people—in Max Weber's term, a pariah or guest people. For most of Jewish history from 586 B.C.E., the vast majority of Jews lived as guest peoples, operating under a system which began in Babylonia but was continually refined in the centuries which followed.

With the advent of Christianity and Islam, which were themselves to some extent ritually and theologically segregated groups, the Jews found themselves more isolated by society than they had been in the more open Greco-Roman environment. In Christian and Muslim societies, the position of the Jews was legally demeaned and limited. Jews were excluded from many normal avenues of expression both to demean them because they would not adhere to the religious "truth" and to prevent them from unduly tainting the new revelation. To compensate for this change in their social situation, the Jews reasserted their belief in their own role and superiority and drew within themselves, not because of outside pressure but to keep themselves pure and to prevent contamination from without. They would remain in readiness for God's redemption through His appointed Messiah. Several individuals claimed to be the Messiah during this period, especially the very widely accepted Turkish Jew, Shabbatai Zevi, in the seventeenth century. Unfortunately he proved to be only one more of a rather long series of false Messiahs.

Other peoples have also been identified as pariah or guest peoples or, in more clearly economic terminology, as "marginal trading peoples." The social specialness of various peoples was also expressed in their economic roles and experiences. Howard Becker, who apparently was not aware of Weber's formulations, characterized marginal trading peoples as possessing a high degree of expedient rationality, emotional aloofness toward out-groups, and a considerable measure of economic internationalism ("wherever my economic good is found, there is my country"). Besides the Jews, he includes in this category Christian Armenians in Turkey, Parsees in India, and Chinese and Greeks living outside their own countries. While some of these peoples use religion for the same purpose as the Jews, all are characterized by a slow accumulation of folkways and mores, catastrophic changes involving wars, migrations, rise of charismatic leaders, and rationalization of essentially non-rational values.[1] Miriam Beard would add to this list Quakers, Huguenots, and the border Scots, who traded along Hadrian's wall in Roman days and later, as staunch Presbyterians, served as agents between Catholics and Anglicans. The children of all of these religious pariahs married with co-religionists to keep their wealth intact, thereby increasing their fortunes over several generations.[2] Even in the Christian world, specialized Christian merchants would function as a guest people. This was the case with the Caursines, who also dealt in money under the protection of princes. They, however, could eat with Christians and marry their daughters.[3]

The economic situation in which the Jews found themselves as a result of their milieu was determined by factors intrinsic to the Jewish experience, and extrinsic to their society. General and frequent hostility between Christian and Muslim states, located as they were on both shores of the Mediterranean, helped make necessary an intermediate people who could serve as agents of trade. The Jews, as outsiders in both societies, could serve this role admirably. In addition the continued use of Hebrew as the liturgical language meant that they possessed a common tongue for negotiations wherever other Jews lived. The fellowship which Jews felt for one another also facilitated the extension of credit and the acceptance of various agreements essential to commerce.

The very fact that the Jews were engaged in international commerce gave them the experience necessary to develop new techniques to solve unique problems. In this way they developed promissory notes, inserting in them the clause of power of attorney, so that the notes could be used eventually as negotiable securities. They also saw the necessity of the legal enforcement of their claims against tardy debtors. Gradually, these and other practices found their way into the legal codes of the general community.[4]

What appears to be Jewish pioneering in economic affairs in Europe was often the migration of commercial ideas carried by migrating Jews from more advanced places, usually from Muslim to Christian lands or from one Christian land to another. At times it was physical danger which drove the Jews. But some of the Jewish migration from Italy may have been a matter of leaving an area where they were out-expertized by Italians who were also better situated socially. The Jews would then go to a region which was relatively backward, only to be displaced once again as the newly developed society grew and became sophisticated. Then they would leave voluntarily or, more usually, be expelled with the religious rationalization that a Jew was not to succeed at the expense of a Christian.[5]

The Jews also served as economic pioneers and avant-gardists. There were certain essential commercial tasks which for a time Christian doctrines prohibited Christians from practicing, particularly loaning on interest. In addition to the fact that Jews came from more advanced areas, many of the various restrictions placed on them, particularly with regard to holding land and slaves, caused them to be more adventuresome in finding opportunities for material survival. In the Carolingian period the terms *Jew* and *merchant* were almost interchangeable. There was little place for commerce in the early medieval town, which was markedly agrarian. Yet a community with an abundance of goods would find merchants useful as agents of exchange. The Jews not only performed a necessary economic function, but they developed what was almost a guardianship over trade.[6] One scholar attributes the origin and development of the burgher class in northwestern Europe to the presence of Jews. Gradually, their non-Jewish associates and neighbors learned this highly complicated and unusually lucrative way of life. Once this was achieved there would be no need for Jews.[7]

With the growth of the mercantile spirit and enterprise in Europe, particularly in the cities, from the period of the crusades on, Jews were displaced from favorable positions. Competition came from the church as it lent money under the guise of *mons pietata,* but more so from the emerging middle class, which was the chief bearer of the intolerant combination of nationalism and religion. The Jews were seen primarily as competitors who could easily be eliminated. The states that unified first expelled Jews first. These included Spain, France, and England. Fortunately the two large multinational states of Lithuania-Poland and the Ottoman Empire welcomed numbers of Jews.

The merchant craft guilds were another device utilized to displace Jews and to keep them from possible areas of involvement. Permeated with Christian forms in their economic and social activities, the guilds excluded Jews, who were thereby cut off from the privileges which these mercantile corporations enjoyed. As more and more Christians entered such activities as moneylending, Jews suffered from other disadvantages. In the enforcement of money obligations, Christians were officially given preference under the law. Creditors were legally bound to pay Christians first, even to the exclusion of a Jew.[8]

Wilhelm Roscher admirably summarizes this entire process.

> The Jews, through their talents and activities, have in every age and in every type of economy fulfilled a certain economic function. They were needed and used for certain pioneering functions. This need existed as long as the majority of the population had either no interest or no ability for such economic services. As soon as they learned to satisfy this need themselves, the mission of the Jew was finished. Medieval policy toward the Jews may be said to have followed a direction almost inverse to the general economic trend. As soon as people became mature enough to perform that function themselves they tried to emancipate themselves from such guardianship over their trade, aften in bitter conflict. The persecutions of the Jews in the later Middle Ages are thus to a great extent a product of commercial jealousy. They are connected with the rise of a national merchant class.[9]

Kisch, in analyzing the laws of this period, finds this evolution verified. The changing laws always supported Christians when they were ready to enter activities which had been performed by Jews. Religious feelings reinforced the economic needs of Christians and the church.[10]

Where the Jews were displaced but not expelled, their economic position degenerated. From moneylending with personal property as security, they entered pawnbroking, which in turn led to dealing in second-hand goods, their main occupation in the fifteenth century. While recognizing the economic role of the Jews in the Middle Ages, Miriam Beard feels that it has been grossly exaggerated. Her research and that of others indicates that the dominant figures in international finance from the thirteenth to the seventeenth century were Christians. Rather than Jews as the crafty wizards who overpowered simple gentiles, the opposite is nearer the truth. That Jews attracted greater folk animosity than Christians was due to their being humbler and dealing more with the plain people, making them easier targets for enmity.

Although the Jews long maintained a strong position in commerce and industry in Spain, they could not win a prominent position in northern Germany among the Hanseatics, nor could they effectively compete with the natives of Florence. By 1200, Italian bankers were pushing them out of England and France, which were even more backward. More advanced methods of finance capitalism were introduced by the Florentines, who needed no instruction in gauging and gain. The Jews seldom dominated where the Florentines were in commerce. Florentine superiority was based in part on access to sources of finance denied the Jews—the church and industry. When the Jews were squeezed by English kings, it was usually to pay debts contracted by some Italian consortium, such as the Florentine Della Scala and Dalboragal families, which lent the British crown half a million gold lira in 1226. As security they demanded a lien on most of the royal income, including revenue from the king's forest and the tax on the Jews.[11]

The complex problem of the prohibition of lending on interest was eventually solved by the different branches of Christianity. Jewish law, based on blood brotherhood and the exclusion of the foreigner from special consideration, forbade taking interest from a brother, but not from a foreigner (Deut. 23:19 f.). Christianity and Western morality solved this problem by refusing to concede that God could authorize treating the "other" differently than a brother.[12] In Christianity, though, brother and other were assimilated into what became a universal otherhood. In modern capitalism all are brothers in being equally others, and so interest could be exacted from all. A commercial society required this conclusion. Robert de Curzon (d. 1219), in his argument with St. Ambrose, disagreed that Jews alone could be usurers by stating that Christians were really *gerim* and protected by Jewish law (Exod. 22:12, Lev. 25:35 ff.).[13] Martin Luther approved of usury as the method devised by God to punish gentiles.[14] Also, since Jews disobeyed God, usury could be used by gentiles against them. Calvin carried this line of reasoning further by stating that the Deuteronomic law must be applied to profit Christians rather than to justify the exploitation of Christians by Jews.[15] Christianity thus enabled Christians to profit more efficiently by making it possible for them to take interest from all members of society, including their own co-religionists. As a result, Christianity became more suited to the developing capitalistic, money-oriented society.

There were several ramifications for proselyting in this environment. Separations based on religion tended to keep Jews, Christians, and Muslims apart, yet there was considerable conversion to Judaism. The larger number of converts probably came from the ranks of Jewish slaves. Non-Jews may have been attracted in some locales by the higher level of Jewish culture and for economic benefit. Others used conversion as a means of protest against their original society. Of course Jews converted to Christianity and Islam for similar reasons.

This same milieu would also militate against Jews seeking or even accepting converts. It was dangerous to individuals and, on occasion, to entire Jewish communities. Also, the economic specialization which the Jews were increasingly forced into limited the number of Jews who could support themselves in a given community. This may have been behind the attempt of a Jew who tried to take over a tax concession possessed by a convert. The Jew was harshly censured, it being pointed out that it was a grave sin to harm the interests of a proselyte.[16] Specialness of enterprise could work for a group only if it did not get too large. Growth would necessitate some migration or expansion into new economic fields, threatening the majority group and further endangering the guest people. All these pressures, in all probability, kept the number of converts relatively small. People thought in religious terms, and most life needs for most people were expressed through religion. Increasingly, as the Middle Ages ended, religion played a less important role in society.

PART IV

GROUP CONVERSION TO JUDAISM

16
Introduction

FROM ANCIENT times religion was utilized as a primary instrument of organizing people. Loyalty to a regime was often signified by loyalty to a god or set of gods through the practice of rites and rituals. While what amounts to mass conversion to Judaism took place for a variety of reasons when numbers of individuals converted, there are several instances of conversion by whole peoples or significant segments of peoples. In at least one of these cases, the conversion of the Idumeans and Itureans, the conversion came about through force asserted by Jewish conquerors. In most of the other instances discussed in this section, conversion to Judaism was probably initiated by the gentiles themselves for some specific purpose.

The sources for many of these group conversions are scanty. Some of them are simply not mentioned in Jewish sources, and others entered Jewish literature only long after the event is purported to have taken place. It is not clear, on firm historical grounds, whether some of these conversions actually took place, and, if they did, just why the particular group converted. For these reasons, much of the material in this section, and the interpretations based on the material, is tentative. It does show, however, that until the modern period conversion to a new religion continued to be, for many, the primary method of organizing their lives and of expressing dissatisfaction with their lot and their former religion.

17

The Idumeans and Itureans

DURING the period of the resurgence of Jewish national independence under the Hasmonean dynasty (167–37 B.C.E.), several neighboring peoples were conquered. Among these were the Idumeans, the Itureans, and the Moabites. The conquered peoples were offered a choice—either associate with the Jewish conquerors through conversion to Judaism or undergo expulsion and liquidation. Whichever alternative was accepted, the Jewish hold on their territories would be consolidated. The Hasmoneans explained that the holiness of the land of Israel must be re-instituted, and this could only be achieved if all its inhabitants were adherents of Judaism. The Moabites refused to convert and were destroyed. The Idumeans and the Itureans converted.

Virtually all that is known of these events is found in the works of Josephus. The origin of the Idumeans is traced back to Esau, who took up residence on Mount Seir, where he ruled over Idumea, calling the land Edom. The terms Edom and Idumea are interchangeable in Josephus. The relationship between the Jews and the Idumeans goes back to the time of the exodus, when Edom refused to let Moses and the Israelites pass through its territory. Later, the tribe of Simeon was apportioned the part of Idumea that bordered Egypt and Arabia. Saul defeated the Idumeans, as did David through his officer Abishai, slaying 18,000. David then occupied their land and collected tribute. Solomon took some of his wives from them. Hadad, an Idumean, rebelled against him (1 Kings 11:14). Jehoshaphat compelled the Idumean king to join him in a campaign against Moab. Considerably later, Darius commanded the Idumeans to return a number of villages they had taken from the Jews. Then came the confrontation with the Maccabees. Josephus writes: "And [Judas] falling upon the descendants of Esau at Akrabatene, killed many of them and took their spoil." War against them continued with the Jews taking Hebron, destroying all its fortifications and towers. John Hyrcanus I subdued the entire land, permitting the Idumeans to continue to occupy it as long as they had themselves circumcised and followed and remained loyal to the laws of the Jews. This is a clear exposition of the kind of process that followed the first conquest and occupation of Canaan by Joshua and his successors. The land was to be unified politically through a degree of religious conformity.

Josephus then goes on to tell of the continuing relationship between the two peoples. That Idumeans were involved in the politics of the Jewish state is seen from the appointment of Antipater as governor of Idumea by Alexander Janneus. His son, also named Antipater, was a friend of John Hyrcanus. A man of great wealth, he sought to extend his influence through gifts and alliances, and was deeply involved in palace power politics. He was married to Cypros, of a distinguished Arab family. Herod was one of her sons.

This same Herod was proclaimed king of the Jewish state. Protests were brought before the Romans since Herod was both a commoner and an Idumean, that is, a half-Jew. Many felt that one of the royal family should be king.

Not all Idumeans identified with the Jews and their state. Costobarus, one of the leading Idumeans, whose ancestors had been priests of Koze, was appointed governor of Idumea and Gaza by Herod. After killing Joseph, the former husband of his sister Salome, Herod gave her in marriage to Costobarus. Operating from this position of power, Costobarus sought to gain independence for Idumea so that the Idumeans could give up Judaism and return to their own customs. In pursuit of this goal, he told Cleopatra that Idumea had belonged to her ancestors and that she had the right to ask Marc Antony for it. Antony refused the request and informed Herod, who planned to kill Costobarus. His sister and mother intervened.

During the rebellion against Rome the Zealots enlisted the aid of the Idumeans, who they felt would respond since they were a "turbulent and disorderly people, ever on the alert for commotion and delighting in revolutionary changes." They did indeed respond, with at least 20,000 troops, fully identifying themselves as Jews. However, they seem to have operated as a separate, identifiable group with their own leaders. They made peace separately with Titus (Josephus, *Jewish Antiquities* 2. 1, 6; 4. 76; 5. 82; 6. 129; 7. 109; 8. 191, 200, 203; 9. 30,

97; 11. 61; 12. 328, 353; 13. 257 f., 396; 14. 8 ff., 121, 403; 15. 254–66; 17. 254; *Jewish War,* 4. 224, 231, 274, 353; 6. 378 ff.).

Much less is noted of the Itureans, a people living in the Lebanon, with the Phoenician hinterland on the west and the country south of Damascus on the east. Aristobulus I fought against them in 105–104 B.C.E., forcing those who wished to remain to be circumcised and live in accord with the laws of the Jews. At the time of the Roman conquest they were still considered an uncivilized robber tribe with good bowmen. Caesar used them in his African war. Most of them lived at Mount Lebanon, although at the time of Aristobulus, some were also found in the Galilee. The petty states of Chalcis and Abilene were carved out of what had been Iturea. The Itureans were related to Itur, one of the sons of Ishmael (Gen. 25:15, 1 Chron. 1:31, 5:19). The earliest mention of them is by Eupolemus (mid-2nd cent. B.C.E.), a Jewish Hellenist writer, who lists them among the tribes which fought against David.[1]

Zeitlin believes that the Idumeans were co-religionists of the Jews but remained a separate though kindred nation. He would not apply the term *ethnos* to them since they did not assimilate with Jews to become one ethnic group.[2] For this reason he would not translate Josephus' *homophulon* as "kinsmen" but as "co-religionist" (*Jewish War* 1. 2). Indicative of the large number of such persons, Josephus notes that 1,100,000 perished during the conquest by the Romans, most of them *homophulon,* who had come to Jerusalem for Passover and were caught up by the war.[3] Josephus comments further that Herod, though neither his father nor his mother was of the Jewish race, was considered a full Jew. His grandson Agrippa read from the Torah on Sukkot.[4] This was apparently the last instance of Jews forcing a people to convert. Until modern times they would not again be in the power position necessary for such an action.

18
Adiabene

THE CONVERSION of the royal family of Adiabene, and perhaps a considerable portion of the populace, in the first century C.E., received favorable comment both in Josephus and the Talmud. It seems that Izates and his mother, Helene, went out of their way to make a favorable impression on the Jewish establishment. The following details are taken primarily from Josephus.

Adiabene was located on a line halfway between Antioch and the southern shore of the Caspian Sea, south of Armenia. It was a considerable distance due east of Anatolia. King Monobazus I of Adiabene married his sister, Helene, who bore him a son, Izates, which may mean "genius" or "godly being." While Monobazus had other wives and children, Izates was the favorite and destined to succeed his father on the throne. To safeguard him from the envy of his half-brothers, he was sent to Charax Spasini, a small state located between the mouths of the Tigris and Euphrates rivers near the Persian Gulf. Subsequently, his father placed him in charge of the district of Carron, from which he was called to be king when his father died.

While Izates was in Charax Spasini, a Jewish merchant named Ananias was brought to his attention by women in his court who had been attracted to Judaism. Izates was converted by Ananias, who accompanied him when he returned to his homeland. During the same period his mother had been converted by another Jewish merchant, Hananya. Izates sought to formalize his conversion through circumcision. His mother and Ananias opposed this lest the act alienate too many of his own people. Ananias, perhaps, fearing that he would bear the blame for any complications, indicated that full adherence to Judaism was more important than circumcision. A Galilean Jew named Eleazar, however, urged the circumcision, which was then immediately performed.

The Adiabeneans did many things to indicate their loyalty to Judaism. When Helene went to live in Jerusalem in 46 or 47 c.e., she took a large sum of money with which she bought grain and other necessities for the famine-struck people. When Izates learned of the famine he sent more funds. Helene remained in Jerusalem until 55 c.e., when Izates' death caused her to return to Adiabene. She died shortly after her son. Monobazus II, who succeeded his brother as king, sent his mother's and brother's bones to be buried in three pyramids which they had built in Jerusalem. Other references indicate that Adiabeneans had palaces in Jerusalem. A number of Adiabeneans fought in the Jewish ranks during the first revolt, defending Jerusalem against the Romans. After the Jewish defeat, "on the same day the sons and brothers of king Izates, who were joined by many of the eminent townsfolk, entreated Caesar to grant them a pledge of protection." Titus apparently did this, eventually bringing them in chains to Rome as hostages for the allegiance of their country (*Jewish Antiquities* 20. 17–96; *Jewish War* 2. 388 f., 520; 4. 567; 5. 252 f., 474; 6. 355 f.). Little more is heard of the Jewish kingdom after its defeat by Trajan in 116. The house of Monobazus seems not to have returned to its homeland after the threat passed. Perhaps it was replaced by another noble family which found it possible to seize the throne because the conversion and subsequent policies of its predecessors had alienated the population.

It is not entirely certain why the royal family of Adiabene converted. Clearly, they were attracted to the religion itself. They went farther in their devotion to Jerusalem and its inhabitants than other groups of converts. Geography helped somewhat in this. Yet there may also have been a political and economic motivation.

Because of its location, Adiabene was caught between Parthia and the Roman Middle Eastern provinces. Dynastic difficulties in Parthia and imperial problems in Rome inevitably affected Adiabene, as did the frequent attempts of both empires to neutralize and conquer one another.[1] For this reason it would have made excellent sense for Adiabene to attempt to become more independent of its neighboring empires.

One method of accomplishing this would be through winning the political allegiance of the Jews of the area. With any luck, the sizable Jewish population of Palestine could then serve as Adiabene's western frontier, removing Rome from the central region of the potential extended state. Parts of Adiabene itself had established Jewish communities. This was particularly true of Nisibis, a part of Adiabene ceded to Izates by Artabanus of Parthia in 36 C.E. Its Jewish population may have dated back to the exile of Jews from Israel in 722 B.C.E., located as it was in the center of the region of settlement mentioned in the Bible (2 Kings 17:6, 18:11). It was also the center for the collection of Temple offerings from northern Mesopotamia, as Nehardea was in the south. Jews and Jewish dynasties controlled other neighboring areas. During the first century Armenia was ruled by a Jewish dynasty descended from Herod. Other regimes in Chalcis, Cappadocia, Iturea, and Abilene were similarly ruled. Further south in Babylonia there were large numbers of Jews. For a brief period, 20–35, there was an autonomous state ruled by two Jews, Anileus and Asineus. It was formally recognized by the Parthian ruler, Artabanus. Then, of course, there was the support given by the Adiabeneans to the Jewish community of Jerusalem and the armed assistance during the war against Rome.

As a result of all this, the rulers of Adiabene could form a hegemony based on political alliances bolstered by religious ties. It would be bounded by Parthia on the south and east, and Armenia on the north, east, and west. At the time of its conversion the Mesopotamian valley was in a state of unrest. Parthia was weakened by dynastic disputes, and there was no solidly established government in the area south of Armenia excepting for local regimes established by Jews and Greeks in Babylonia. Farther westward, the restiveness of the Jews under the Romans made them possible allies. Adiabene, located as it was between the two large Jewish communities of Palestine and Babylonia, could have seen them as keys to any possible plans for imperial growth. In periods of political instability small states have frequently risen, at least for short periods, to international prominence. Adiabene may have seen its opportunity during the war of 66 against Rome. It may have been felt that a Jewish victory in Palestine would provide the opportunity for a member of the royal family of Adiabene to occupy the Jewish throne. After all, other converts, the descendants of Antipater, sat on the Jewish throne. Moreover, Agrippa II was discredited by his association with Rome and his opposition to the war, while Adiabeneans actively fought against Rome.

Jews in the region could well have had their own reasons for wanting to see such a plan succeed. It would, first of all, vindicate the validity of their religion. Commercial gains would also have resulted through the establishment of a larger state. Both Izates and Helene were converted by Jewish merchants. The unsavory rule of both the Herodians and the Romans would be replaced by a regime which appeared to be fully sympathetic to both Judaism and Jews.[2] Much of this cannot be verified historically, but it seems to fit the pattern of other conversions by ruling families. What is clear is that the royal family of Adiabene converted, was loyal to Judaism, assisted the Jews of Palestine in times of peace and war, and was accepted in glowing terms by official Judaism.[3]

19

Jews in South Arabia and the Conversion of Dhu Nuwas

JEWS AND Arabs have had relationships with each other since antiquity. References in the Bible verify this. Just when organized groups of Jews settled in various parts of Arabia is uncertain, but it has been suggested that fleeing groups took refuge there after the national disasters of 586 B.C.E. and 70 C.E. Only the later date would appear to be valid, because it was not until about 350 C.E. that there is definite evidence of Jewish communities in Arabia. It may be supposed that there was some Jewish contact with southern Arabia in the time of Solomon, who traded in that region, as his legendary connection with the Queen of Sheba suggests. Definite mention of Jews in this area comes from Josephus. "Herod sent to Caesar five hundred chosen warriors whom Aelius Gallus led to the Red Sea." This took place about 25 B.C.E. and ended in disaster (*Jewish Antiquities* 15. 317).

Jewish tribes are known to have been influential in Yathrib, the northwestern Arabian oasis which became the scene of Mohammed's first successes. The names of the Jews of Arabia indicate that they were probably Judaized Arabs. Perhaps their Judaism resulted from the influence of a small number of Jews who had come from Palestine. The Arab historian al-Bakri preserves a tradition that the Jews of Teima prevented the Banu Hishna, a subdivision of the Bali tribe, from entering their fort until they embraced Judaism, which they did. Jews were prominent in northern Arabia and must have exerted a considerable influence on Mohammed.[1] It has been suggested that the Jews attracted attention and converts because their advanced methods of irrigation and cultivation made them successful in agriculture. They also developed arts and crafts new to the area, such as metalworking, dyeing, and the production of fine jewelry. In addition, Judaism itself was attractive because it was so different from the indigenous religions.[2] Some scholars maintain that the practices of the supposed Jewish tribes of northern Arabia were atypical, and that actually they were not authentically Jewish, but because of their monotheistic beliefs were termed Jews by Arab historians. Whether or not this is so, there is no doubt that they were identified as Jews in the Koran.[3]

It is clear, then, that the nature of the Jewish settlement in Arabia is problematic. Our only records of the conversion of Dhu Nuwas, the king of Himyar in southern Arabia, come from Arabic and Christian sources. Apparently he was converted by his father, Abu Kariba, who had converted earlier under the influence of some Jews who assisted him in a campaign against Persia and some of the Arabian provinces of Byzantium. Dhu Nuwas, the last of the Himyarite kings, became a devoted Jew whose zeal alienated many Christian merchants who were crucial to the trade between Arabia and India. A neighboring king, Aidug, defeated Dhu Nuwas, who retaliated by attacking another Christian city, Najran. He besieged the city, giving its inhabitants the alternatives of accepting Judaism or death. They chose the latter and 20,000 were killed. One escaped, seeking aid in Byzantium, which was refused because of the distance, but finding some in Abyssinia, which sent a force of 70,000. This army defeated Dhu Nuwas, who committed suicide by jumping into the sea with his horse.

All of this took place between 520 and 530. Different versions of the story appear in the writings of Arab, Syrian, and Greek historians. The events seem to revolve about the political rivalry between Byzantium and Persia, and the religious rivalry between Christianity, which was just penetrating the area, and Judaism and paganism, which existed side by side and represented traditional elements. Lending some credence to this is the joint opposition of Jews and pagans to the mission of Theophilus, dispatched by Constantius (349–61).[4] The Christian sources feature persecution and martyring of Christians. The Muslims weave great detail into their narratives, which seem contrived for the most part, and appear to uphold the indigenous population against the invaders.[5]

Attempts to interpret the political problems of the area on the basis of the conversion and career of Dhu Nuwas are varied. Baron sees the treacherous extermination of the Christian community of Najran as merely an excuse for Abyssinian intervention. From this point of view,

Dhu Nuwas was the leader of a movement seeking liberation from Abyssinian supremacy. He sought the assistance of the pro-Persian Lakhmids and possibly of Persia itself, but his effort ended in dismal failure. The Christian Abyssinians could count on the support of Byzantium, which provided the ships to transport the Abyssinian troops to southern Arabia. At the same time the Jewish king received no material aid from the Sassanians. Anarchy at home immobilized the Persians. This episode may have caused Judaism to be identified with resistance to Abyssinian domination. It may also have served to spread Jewish teachings throughout Arabia, and thus was part of the process leading to Mohammed's mission.[6]

Another suggested interpretation views the situation as one growing out of the struggle between Persia and Byzantium for strategically important land routes and sea lanes. Byzantium, particularly, sought the natural products of the area and the guarantee of free passage to India. To gain these she launched a carefully planned effort to dominate the area politically, economically, and culturally, through encouragement of the Abyssinians. Persia's policy was to prevent Byzantine expansion in the area. Because she sought little more than this, Persian assistance to Dhu Nuwas was considerably less than Byzantine assistance to Abyssinia. In the end Dhu Nuwas was virtually alone in his struggle and was defeated.[7]

Margoliouth concluded from his studies that the Jewish influence was exaggerated or totally contrived for Christian propagandistic purposes. The Christian material was then picked up by Arabic historians, who embellished it for their own purposes.[8] He notes that two ancient historians do not mention any conversion to Judaism. Philostorgius (ca. 425) writes that in his time the Himyarites practiced circumcision on the eighth day, but sacrificed to the sun, moon, and local deities. Theodorus Lector, writing at the beginning of the sixth century, states that the Queen of Sheba made some converts to Judaism, but their descendants reverted to paganism and were converted to Christianity at the time of Anastasius (491–518). He says nothing of Jews living in the region at the time, nor does he mention a Jewish king.[9]

Once again there are several traditions of the conversion of a royal figure, and presumably a considerable portion of his people, although in widely divergent accounts. At the very least, it may be concluded that the possibility of conversion by large groups of people was not discounted by either Christian or Muslim historians.

20

The Conversion of the Berbers of North Africa

TRADITIONS of widespread conversion to Judaism in North Africa go back to the time of the earliest church fathers of that area. The traditions seem to relate to converts from among the inhabitants of the Roman coastal cities and adjacent communities rather than the Berbers of the interior. For our purposes, the category of Berber includes all those inhabitants of the Maghreb who maintained their distinctive ethnic identity, language, and customs. After the Arab conquest, increasing numbers of them became Arabized through adopting the language and urban culture of the invaders. Although this process began early in the eighth century, it is estimated that between one-third and one-half of the people of the region still remain Berbers. Even before the time of the Romans, the native peoples of North Africa were confronted with cultural influences of all kinds, including that of Jews. The Jewish influence resulted in such a large number of conversions that upwards of one-half of the Jews of Morocco are considered to be descended from Berbers who converted to Judaism in the pre-Muslim period.

Some think Jews entered North Africa with Phoenician traders as early as 1000 B.C.E. Others place their entrance in significant numbers after the disasters in Palestine of 586 B.C.E. and 70 C.E. It seems certain that many went there from Spain during the persecution of Jews under the Visigoths. Others, no doubt, accompanied the Arab forces invading North Africa and Spain. Large numbers fled Spain once again during the reconquest by the Christians, culminating with the expulsion of hundreds of thousands of Jews and Muslims in 1492.

Conversion to Judaism by Berbers was recorded for the first time in the twelfth century by the Arabic historian Al-Idrisi, who writes of the region south of present-day Morocco. Ibn Abi Zar, who lived in the fourteenth century, is the next literary source. He writes of two tribes of the Berber Banu Zanata, living near Fez, that were a mixture of Muslims, Christians, Jews, and pagans. The primary source for the tradition of Berber conversion to Judaism is the great Tunisian historian Ibn Khaldun (1336–1406), who wrote some 750 years after the events he described. His comments on this subject are very carefully expressed: "It is also possible that some of these tribes of Berbers adhered to the Jewish religion which they had adopted from the children of Israel at the time of the expansion of their kingdom to the vicinity of Syria and their rule over it. This may have been the case with the Jarawa, the people of the Aures Mountains, the tribe of Kahina, who was killed by the Arabs at the beginning of the conquest." [1] Ibn Khaldun mentions other tribal groups that may have converted in the region from the mountains on the border between Tripolitania and Tunisia westward to central Morocco.

Other medieval historians and travelers in the area perpetuated the tradition that many of the Jews were Berber converts. As noted, Jews lived in the Maghreb from an early period. The string of Jewish communities from Libya to the western Sudan is indicative of the vastness of the area traveled by Jewish merchants. Stories of Jewish kingdoms also began to circulate, the first by Eldad Ha-Dani, who was in Tunisia in 880 and then went on to Spain.[2] Legends of the Ten Tribes led to stories of Judaized Negroes as well as Berbers in the Sudan.[3]

The outstanding critic of the vast literature relating to this subject is H. Z. Hirschberg. He suggests that these stories originated among Jews seeking to enhance their prestige among their neighbors and then assumed an "independent existence," even serving as weapons against the Jews.[4] Arabs could also have begun such traditions as a means of indicating their superiority over Berber converts to Islam by pointing out their weakness in having previously converted to Judaism. The traditions were further enhanced by the fact that the influence of the Jews living throughout this region probably led the indigenous population to adopt some Jewish customs. The voluntary and forced ethnic and religious assimilation of Jews to the Muslim population might well have led to traditions of Judaized Berbers converting to Islam. Also, after living together with the Berbers for so long, Jews may have become so integrated into Berber society that they came to be considered Judaized

Berbers themselves. The mutual cultural exchange between Jews and Berbers may have continued well after the Arab conquest in those regions where Islam had not penetrated. Hirschberg's major argument against a widespread conversion of Berbers to Judaism rests on the complete absence of any penetration of Berber languages into Jewish literature. In addition, the rabbinic literature of the time in North Africa contains no indication whatsoever that any of the Jews it was concerned with were Judaized Berbers.[5]

An outstanding anthropologist, L. Cabot Briggs, who spent many years studying Saharan communities, including an extended period among the Jews of the Mzab, a Saharan region of Algeria, came to different conclusions. "In short, we get the impression of an old Berber population that swallowed up a handful of Jewish missionaries from Palestine, broke up their genotypes by the simple process of torrential dilution, and scattered the isolated genes among the newly hybrid but still overwhelmingly Berber population."[6] Briggs agrees with the conclusions of earlier students who held that a great proportion of the Jews of North Africa were Judaized Berbers, conclusions based also on blood studies.[7] Several other students of the Judaizing of the Berbers basically agree with these conclusions.[8]

It is clear that there is no absolute proof of large-scale Berber conversions to Judaism. However, while they cannot be verified historically, traditions going back for centuries and continuing into contemporary times lend some credence to the argument. Other instances of mass conversions to Judaism, such as those of the Falashas and the Khazars, also did not find their way into the contemporary Jewish literature. In any event, the presence of considerable numbers of Jews among the Berbers of North Africa seems to have resulted in broad assimilation of Jewish practices and ideas. This more closely approximates the assimilation of the indigenous population of Canaan during the biblical period than formal conversion with the enactment of rites. But it seems clear that Judaism was transferable to an alien population and was attractive to it.

21
The Conversion of the Khazars

THE BEST-KNOWN mass conversion of a people to Judaism was that of the Khazars, a Turkic people who occupied the territory between the Black and the Caspian Seas. While this conversion is mentioned in Jewish, Muslim, and Christian literature as early as the tenth century, there are many contradictions regarding the date of the conversion, how it took place, and the kind of Judaism the Khazars practiced. Complete reviews of all the available materials on the Khazars have been written. Yet before these questions can be answered, new sources will have to be discovered.

The oldest source which tells of the conversion in a rather complete form is the correspondence between a Spanish-Jewish personality, Hasdai ibn Shaprut, and Joseph, king of the Khazars, which took place no later than 961. In response to a letter from Ibn Shaprut, Joseph related the conversion of the Khazars at the time of Bulan, about 750. Sometime later, it is related, a descendant or grandson of Bulan, Obadiah, introduced a reformation, and perhaps at this time Rabbinic Judaism was introduced. Joseph's letter includes most of the details known about the conversion. As early as 1826 doubt concerning the authenticity of Joseph's reply was raised.[1] A. N. Poliak calls the entire correspondence a literary fiction produced by Rabbinic Judaism, which seized the story of the Khazar conversion to aid in its struggle against the Karaites. The account of the debate at the Khazar court was used to promote Rabbinic Judaism.[2]

Another version of the conversion which is more acceptable to many scholars is that related in the Cambridge Document, a Hebrew manuscript of less than 100 lines, probably dating from the twelfth century. It was among the materials from the Cairo Genizah and was first published by Solomon Schechter in 1912.[3] In this account, the conversion of the Khazars stems from the presence in Khazaria of Jews who had come there from Byzantium to escape persecution. Following the death of one of the Khazar kings, the country's bravest general was selected as his successor. It turned out that he was a Jew. A disputation between representatives of Judaism, Christianity, and Islam followed, with Judaism the victor. It was declared the official religion of the Khazar state, and eventually almost the whole population of Khazaria converted.

In spite of the contradictions between these and other sources, and the varied opinions of the many scholars who have considered the problems, Dunlop concludes that the "existence of the Khazars and the fact that at one time they were Jews are beyond suspicion, on the overwhelming testimony of many independent sources."[4] He further holds that "sometime before 730, the leading Khazars may have come under the influence of Judaism."[5]

About this time the Khazars engaged in a successful campaign against the Arabs, but the situation was reversed in 737 when Islam was imposed on the khaqan and his people. Following a religious debate about 740, shortly after the Arabs withdrew, the khaqan accepted a modified Judaism. About 800, a descendant of the khaqan accepted Rabbinic Judaism.[6] The conversion, according to J. B. Bury, was chiefly opportunistic and politically motivated.

> There can be no question that the ruler was actuated by political motives in adopting Judaism. To embrace Mohammedanism would have made him the spiritual dependent of the Caliphs, who attempted to press their faith on the Khazars, and in Christianity lay the danger of his becoming an ecclesiastical vassal of the Roman Empire. . . . [Judaism] elevated him above the heathen barbarians, and secured him against interference of Caliph or Emperor. He allowed the mass of his people to abide in their heathendom and worship their idols.[7]

The influence of Jews in this area is not surprising since they had been there long before the Khazars. Historians of Armenia and Georgia record Jewish settlements in the Caucasus and Transcaucasus soon after the destruction of Judea in 586 B.C.E. By the end of the fourth century B.C.E., cities in Armenia had large Jewish populations. In the fifth and sixth centuries C.E., these populations were augmented by large groups of Jews fleeing the persecution of the church in Byzantium.[8] Another suggested source of Jewish influence in this region is from a group of "mountain Jews" known as the Judeo-Tats. They apparently left Palestine after 586 B.C.E. and migrated to northern Persia. When the Khazars were contending with the Persian Sassanians for Derbent, these Jews spread north to the Khazar-dominated Transcaucasus region among the Dogestan mountain tribes. This may have led to their influencing the Khazars toward Judaism.[9]

Several references to conversion to Christianity and Islam, usually under special conditions, make it clear that the Khazar conversion to Judaism was gradual and suffered occasional setbacks. It is not strange that the Jewish accounts of the conversion would view it as a single impressive event in which Judaism triumphed over its rivals. However, this simply does not seem to have been the case. It is amazing, in light of the fact that the great powers of the period were promoting other faiths, that Judaism should have had any success at all. The social role of religion was victorious over what may have appeared more politic or prudent action.

At least two instances of conversion to Islam are recorded. The first took place in 737 when the Khazars were defeated by Marwan. In consequence of this defeat, the Khazars were offered the option of conversion, which they accepted. This had become a method by which conquering Muslims controlled subject peoples. Apparently the Khazars did not remain Muslims for long. A second instance occurred in the late 960s when the Khazars called for assistance from Khworizm to hold off attacking Russians. The condition demanded by Khworizm was conversion to Islam. The Khazars acceded to the condition. After this time no mention is made of an independent Jewish state.

Khazar relations with Byzantium were often close. Just how close they could be is illustrated by the marriage of the son of Leo III, the future Constantine V, to the khaqan's daughter, Irene, in 733. While Khazar dress and customs were introduced into the court in Constantinople, Byzantine statesmen, for their part, followed the time-honored tradition of Eastern Roman diplomacy by attempting to consolidate the political alliance by converting the Khazars to Christianity. Christianity seems to have spread through Khazaria in the eighth century, partly from the Crimea. While there were plans to establish a missionary church network throughout Khazaria, there is no evidence that it was ever put into operation.[10] A second attempt to implant Christianity is recorded as having taken place in 860, when, at the request of the khaqan, Michael III sent a priest, Constantine, to Khazaria to explain the Christian faith. It seems that his efforts were rewarded with 200 baptisms. The khaqan's request may have been related to some specific political event wherein the assistance of Byzantium was desired.[11]

These occurrences would indicate that Bury was quite correct in seeing politics as at least one of the primary motivating factors in the religious activities of the Khazars. Essential to understanding the role which Judaism might have had for the Khazars is some knowledge of their history and geopolitical problems. Little is known of their early history. Emerging in the area about 550, perhaps subject to the western Turks, they were part of the general rise of Turkish power. Around 630 they were strong enough to conquer Tiflis and march against Persia. By the second half of the seventh century they were fully independent. They were at least partially nomadic, occupying territory between the Volga and the coastal area of the Caucasus. Once allied with the Bulgars to the west, they later expanded at their expense westward to the Don and Kuban rivers. When they reached the Black Sea they came into direct contact with Byzantium and its political and military power as well as its much higher culture. From 642 on, another great military force, the Arabs, came into the area. Conflict with them was periodic. But for the presence of the Khazars, with their military prowess, the Muslims would have overwhelmed Constantinople centuries before they actually did. It is probably for this reason that Byzantine relations with the Khazars were relatively close, although Byzantium was also a potential threat to Khazaria. Already noted was the marriage of children of the two royal families in 733. This was followed by the great Byzantine victory over the Arabs in 740 with Khazar assistance, a victory which cleared western Asia Minor of Arabs.

In 833, indicative of both the continued close relations between the Byzantines and the Khazars and the growing Byzantine interest in the region, Byzantine engineers built a fort for the Khazars at Sarkel at the mouth of the Don. Increasingly threatened by Bulgaria and by Russia, which first attacked Constantinople on June 18, 860, Byzantium continued to use the power of Khazaria.[12] Earlier, in 695, Justinian II was dethroned and exiled to the capital of Khazaria.[13] The Khazars also were helpful in supplying gold from the Urals and silk from China, which helped Byzantium to adjust its economy after the loss of Syria and Egypt to the Arabs.[14] Gradually, due partially to the conversion of the Khazars but also to their declining power and the arrival in the Pontic steppes of the Pechenegs, who could take on the defensive role played by the Khazars, relations with Byzantium cooled. This was during the tenth century, when the effective power of the Khazars came to an end with their crushing defeat by Svjatoslav of Kiev in 965.

The Khazars were caught in a region of great turmoil. Old empires sought to maintain themselves and even expand. New empires were rising. At the same time unsophisticated peoples with considerable military prowess were establishing themselves. Among the latter were the Khazars, who may have seen in Judaism the solution to two of their most pressing problems. First, it provided a way to elevate themselves culturally by adopting a religion that was far advanced over what they had and a worthy competitor of the two other faiths pressing on them. Second, conversion to Judaism would be a way of declaring their independence from Byzantium and the Caliphate, both of which were defined to a considerable extent in religious terms. This motivation for their conversion is well expressed by Baron.

> Not surprisingly both Byzantium and the Caliphate tried to draw the Khazar empire into their respective orbits, the best method of securing such an alliance being the conversion of the desirable neighbor to one's own faith. But precisely because the Khazars wished to retain their neutrality, they repudiated both Christianity and Islam. To secure further non-interference, one of the Khazar rulers, Bulan, formally adopted the third monotheistic religion, Judaism.[15]

The advantages of conversion may be seen in other areas as well. Conversion would bring them an alliance with the large Jewish population already in the area. These Jews possessed advanced agricultural techniques which would be helpful. An alliance with Jews would also mean that the Khazars could take part in the international trade in which the Radanites were engaged throughout the ninth century. This trade extended from Europe to China, taking advantage of the expansionist policies of the T'ang Dynasty (618–907). The Khazars were in a strategic position to participate in this trade, sitting as they did across the east-west routes.[16] The Khazars were "the Venetians of the Caspian Sea and the Euxine, the organizers of the transit between the two basins, the universal carriers between East and West, and Itil was the meeting place of the commerce of Persia, Byzantium, Armenia, Russia and the Bulgarians of the Middle Volga." [17] Khazar merchants are mentioned throughout the area, including Bagdad, Constantinople, the Danube region, and central Asia.[18]

Several factors came together to bring about the decline and virtual end of the Khazars as a viable force. By the tenth century there was a rebirth of Byzantine military power. Coupled with the decline of the eastern Caliphate, this made the mediatory role of the Khazars unnecessary. The crushing blow, however, seems to have been the rise of Russia. After allowing some Russian fleets into Khazar territory to move against the Arabs, the khaqan considered it essential to keep them from coming down the Volga to the Caspian Sea and outflanking Khazaria. By 965 some forts were captured and the capital, Itil, may have been taken.[19] By 969 Itil was destroyed and the independence of the Khazars was ended. The final end came with the Mongol incursions in the 1250s.[20]

As helpful as Judaism may have been for the Khazars, it obviously did not provide what they required to become an imperial power strong enough to withstand the pressure of their neighbors. Dunlop attributes this to the mixed nature of the Khazar population, which, he feels, was never sufficiently uniform. The diverse peoples of Khazaria—Turks, Slavs, Jews, Arabs, and Finns among others—were separated even more by the conglomeration of religions—Judaism, Christianity, Islam, and paganism. Socially, there was also a mix of cultivators, hunters, nomads, merchants, and soldiers. While other empires were not dissimilar in this respect, apparently sufficient unity and sophistication could not be achieved for the Khazar state to prosper and survive. The cultural base was not raised sufficiently or rapidly enough to hold off the challenges. Added to these factors were Khazaria's limited material resources.[21]

It has been noted that the conversion of the Khazars was gradual and the quality of their Judaism uneven. The Talmud was totally unknown, and only minimal reference to the Bible seems to have been made.[22] The earliest reference to their practicing circumcision and other accepted traditions dates from about 865.[23] While the Khazars were remote from other Jewish centers, it is conjectured that the rather desultory kind of Judaism they practiced was the main reason the major Jewish authorities had little to do with them.[24] This is related to the function of Khazar Judaism and the purposes for which the Khazars apparently converted. The Khazars saw their faith not as an instrument of imperial expansion, as did their Muslim and Christian neighbors, but, rather, as a defensive weapon. This may explain the absence of any missionary attempts as well as their watered-down version of Judaism.[25]

While the Jewish Khazars lasted in one form or another within their own region for some five hundred years, their influence continued thereafter. It is suggested that offshoots of the Khazar community moved into the unsubdued Slavonic lands, ultimately building the great Jewish centers of eastern Europe.[26] A contest between Judaism and Christianity, similar to that which took place in Khazaria, seems to have occurred in Kiev, perhaps precipitated by Khazar-related Jews. In this instance, the king, Latimer of Kiev (980–1015), became a Christian. But Jewish influence continued to be so great that the church continually had to teach the superiority of Christianity over Judaism.[27] In addition, the Karaites of the Taurus were Judaized remnants of the Khazars, as were the Jews of Polesia, where the population of the Ukraine fled in the seventeenth century from the Cossacks. These instances are used to suggest the theory that the early Jewish population of the Ukraine consisted basically of descendants of Judaized Khazars.[28]

A similar view is held by Betulani, who states that the oldest Jewish settlements in Poland were established prior to 963, and were founded by Jewish emigres from the Khazar state. He bases his belief in the early arrival of Jews from Khazaria on the usage by Jews in ancient times of the Khazar word for cemetery, *kawiory*.[29] A Russian Jew tells of meetings with Jewish Cossacks in the tsarist army who had a tradition of direct Khazar descent. Ibn Daud, a twelfth-century chronicler, notes that he was personally acquainted with descendants of the Khazars in Toledo.[30]

Brutzkus maintains that the Khazars exercised a profound influence on Russia. Khazar customs, legal terms, and military and administrative techniques were introduced among a number of Slavic tribes over which the Khazars had power. Using philology, Brutzkus attempts to prove that agriculture, handicrafts, and arts were also brought to Russia through the mediation of the Khazars, who had a major cultural role in the country's early development.[31]

While there is no doubt that a considerable number of Khazars converted to Judaism after 740, almost every aspect of this conversion is questionable. The various Jewish, Christian, and Muslim sources give different versions of the event and its aftermath. Historians and other writers on the subject had their own orientations and purposes, and sought to promote their own causes through references to the Khazar conversion. What seems to be clear iş that the Khazars, or a part of them, converted for reasons of state and to benefit from a culture more advanced than their own. Thus the phenomenon of mass conversion to Judaism took place after the establishment of Christianity and Islam, despite its inherent improbability and the powerful imperiums supporting the other two religions.

22

The Falashas

THE BLACK Jews of Abyssinia, otherwise known as the Falashas, are
without question Jewish. They continue to this time as a large, identifiable group. Yet, as with the southern Arabians, Berbers, and Khazars,
nothing is known of their initiation into Judaism which can be scien-
tifically verified. The phenomenon of conversion to Judaism by masses
of people, for various reasons which are not clearly understood, usually
does not lend itself to clear or easy understanding.

As with all esoteric Jewish communities, theories abound regarding
the origin of the Falashas. They claim that they are descended from the
Jews who accompanied Menelik I, the alleged son of King Solomon
and the Queen of Sheba, to Ethiopia. Added to this is the story that the
queen sent her son back to Jerusalem to be educated and that, when he
eventually returned home, he was accompanied by Jews who subsequently married native women. Another tradition maintains that among
the Jews who fled Palestine in the face of the Assyrian and Babylonian
invasions and went to Egypt, some continued up the Nile and established themselves in Ethiopia. Zephaniah 3:10, "From beyond the rivers
of Ethiopia My suppliants, even the daughter of My dispersed, shall
bring My offering," indicates a community there. According to one tradition, when Christianity was introduced into Ethiopia by Frumentius
about 331, half the population of the land was already Jewish. It is also
said that when Solomon's fleet was sailing out of the Red Sea, some of
his men settled in Yemen and others in Ethiopia; further, that during
the Islamic persecution in Arabia, Jews fled to Ethiopia.

From the customs of the Falashas, it is usually concluded that their
form of Judaism is primitive, going back to the period before the compilation of the Talmud. The Falashas rely on the authority of the Bible
and the Book of Jubilees, and from this some scholars have concluded,

115

without real proof, that they are in some way related to the Karaites or the Samaritans. Nothing in Falasha literature or practices bears this out. The very fact of their isolation from the Jewish world and their close contact with the general Ethiopian population could have led to the abandonment of some Jewish customs and the introduction of non-Jewish ones. Their modest material resources might also have led them to abandon some practices, such as sacrifices and synagogues, which were rather costly.

According to most scholarly opinions, a segment of the indigenous Agau population converted to Judaism. How and when this took place is not known. Missionaries may have been sent from the Jewish community in Elephantine in the fifth century B.C.E. or from Yemen. More evidence exists for contacts between Ethiopia and Yemen than between Egypt and Ethiopia. The name Falasha seems to be best explained by the Ethiopic word *fallasa,* which means "to emigrate." The Falashas call themselves "Beta Israel," or House of Israel. Presumably this name was given to them by the older native population. The earliest testimony of the existence of the Falashas comes from Jewish travelers, going back to Eldad Ha-Dani in the ninth century.

Traditions of Hebrew and Jewish influence abound in Abyssinia, but there is almost a complete absence of historical detail and genuine and trustworthy source material. There is, however, considerable linguistic evidence, many religious practices obviously influenced by Judaism, and the strong tradition of the Queen of Sheba. Many scholars accept the tradition that the inhabitants of Abyssinia were partially pagan and partially adherents of a form of Judaized religion prior to the beginning of the Christian conversion in the fourth century. Edward Ullendorff concludes that the Falasha cult comprises a curious mixture of pagan-Judaic-Christian beliefs and ceremonies. Further, he says, the Falashas are descendants of those elements in the Aksunite kingdom who resisted conversion to Christianity.[1] In this respect they are similar to the Khazars, whose conversion to Judaism was in part at least a device for resisting a culture that threatened their identity and perhaps their social role.

The present-day Falasha community numbers between 15,000 and 20,000 and is quite poor. There seems to be little to distinguish Falashas from other Ethiopians in physical appearance. At an earlier time there may have been some economic specialization. They use Amharic, and know no Hebrew. The dietary laws are observed. The presence of monks and nuns is doubtlessly the result of Christian influence. The Falasha Bible is written in Geez and is identical with that of the Christians.

Flad, traveling in Ethiopia in the mid-1850s, stated that there were some 200,000 Falashas. General attrition and conversion to Christianity seem to have dramatically reduced their numbers.[2] Modern organized Jewry has made a few abortive attempts to help these Jews. A considerable number of Falashas have migrated to Israel. In a two-year period, 1970–72, the Sephardic chief rabbi of Israel, Rabbi Ovadia Yosef, converted forty Falashas after they completed a course of instruction. Rabbi Yosef, although convinced of their Jewishness according to Halachah, converted them to satisfy other rabbis.[3]

PART V
AFTER THE
FRENCH REVOLUTION

23
Conversion and Intermarriage

INTRODUCTION

THE SITUATION of the Jews was complicated and mixed after the French Revolution. In the West, especially in the United States, people gained individual rights, constitutionally and legally guaranteed. The Jews suffered under no special legal restrictions. At the same time traditional anti-Semitism continued, becoming general and open in times of political and economic crisis. In the United States anti-Semitism flourished during both the Civil War and the depression in the early thirties. In France it became especially virulent after the Franco-Prussian War, particularly during the Dreyfus affair. Nevertheless, Jews increasingly felt themselves a part of the nations in which they lived, fully participating in the culture of the land.

At the same time Jews suffered grievously in Eastern and Central Europe, which were in turmoil as regimes tottered, especially in Russia, and empires disintegrated, particularly the Ottoman and Austro-Hungarian. As traditional centers toppled, national leaders sought to deflect their citizens from real problems by making the Jews serve the role of social scapegoat. Virulent anti-Jewish activities and outright physical violence against Jews led to a resurgence of long-dormant Jewish national feelings and aspirations.

In this regard the Jews reflected the same nationalistic feelings that were developing among ethnic groups throughout Europe, stimulated by the activities of Napoleon and made possible by the decline of the Ottoman and Austro-Hungarian empires. Jews saw in nationalism not only the opportunity to live their own unique culture fully but also a solution to their millennial problem as victims in societies where they were always a vulnerable minority. In their own state, it was believed, they would be

121

secure and could determine their own destiny. The Dreyfus affair stirred Jewish national aspirations in Western Europe, where Jews had felt more secure. If anti-Semitism could break out so blatantly in the "most civilized" country in the world, where then could Jews feel secure outside their own land?

These cross-currents continued into the twentieth century in an even more dramatic way. While Jews came to feel more secure in such countries as the United States and Germany and England, Communist revolutions in Russia and elsewhere in Eastern Europe took a toll of Jews, who were often portrayed as cosmopolites, inextricably tied to bourgeoise interests. Then, in the aftermath of World War I and the deep depression of the late twenties and early thirties, "racial" anti-Semitism enjoyed a dramatic upsurge, most particularly in Germany.

The destruction of six million Jews during World War II was one of the crucial factors which led finally to the establishment of a Jewish state in the Middle East in 1948. The trauma of the Jewish experience in this period, together with continuous hostility and threats of annihilation by Israel's Arab neighbors, reinforced the millennial siege psychology of the Jews, many of whom often feel themselves to be a people apart from all others, religiously and socially.

Coupled with these feelings of separateness, there is usually a deep longing among Jews to fully identify with the people and culture among whom they live. Whenever general social, political, and economic conditions were favorable, Jews fared well. One symptom of this favorable condition was the increased association between Jews and gentiles, which resulted in increased marriage between the groups. Although the statistics for the nineteenth and twentieth centuries in Europe are open to question, better figures seem to be available for the United States.

While the condition of the Jews in Western Europe and the United States suffered declines from time to time, generally it has been increasingly favorable. Jews have prospered and as a group are among the most favored economically. A correlate of this, at least in the United States, has been a steady increase in the rate of intermarriage, with a concomitant leveling and even decline in the size of the American Jewish community.

It has been suggested from time to time that Judaism ought to develop conversionist programs to compensate for the loss of Jews killed during World War II, those who leave Judaism through disinterest or for other reasons, and the lower Jewish birth rate, which soon may not even equal the death rate. Until now no such program has been developed, blocked by the aversion to proselyting that has been traditional since the Middle Ages; an unwillingness, in fact if not in theory, to accept gentile members; and a general ambivalence to gentiles because of recurring anti-Jewish activities, particularly in Russia and the Middle East. What attempts there have been by rabbis, laymen, and organizations have thus far been ineffective and abortive. While there may have been as many as 7,000 conversions to Judaism annually in recent years, it is estimated that 25,000 conversions a year are required to maintain the size of the American Jewish community.[1] Prior to the Middle Ages, to a limited extent, conversion to Judaism was utilized to maintain the missionary ideology of Judaism as well as its numerical integrity. This solution has yet to be fully utilized on the contemporary scene.

INTERMARRIAGE

THE SURVIVAL of the Jewish people and Judaism has been one of the preoccupations of contemporary Jewry. Significant losses were suffered during World War II. Although no accurate or comprehensive statistics are available, it is also believed that a substantial number of Jews are lost to Judaism through intermarriage, which has reached high levels in the past and is once again increasing. Zeal for conversion on the part of many Jews relates directly to this phenomenon. It is hoped that when a Jew marries a non-Jew, the non-Jew will be encouraged to convert to Judaism. However, the practice varies greatly from individual to individual, family to family, and Reform rabbi to Reform rabbi (virtually no Orthodox or Conservative rabbi will marry a Jew to a non-Jew unless there is a conversion). Because the phenomenon of intermarriage is intimately connected with conversion in modern Jewish communities, it must be carefully studied.

Two systems are operative in the process of intermarriage. The first is the contradiction between the Jewish aspiration to be part of a free and open society, where Jews may live and prosper without facing the discriminations that have historically confronted them, and the subsequent mingling of Jew and non-Jew, often leading to intermarriage. The second, which also affects the relations of Jew and gentile, is the "acculturation to assimilation" pattern.

In the case of the first system the contradiction is more apparent. Jews, individually and collectively, have actively sought out and helped develop social situations where opportunities would not be limited by their religious identity. This has brought them into an increasing number of situations where attributed status has been replaced by earned status, determined by the value of the individual to the society. The openness of such societies makes for greater freedom in other social situations as well. Mates for marriage are increasingly chosen for romantic reasons rather than because they are of the same religion or ethnic group. Individual Jews as well as Jewish organizations find it increasingly difficult to inhibit the resulting intermarriage when, at the same time, they positively identify with the values of freedom, liberalism, and individualism which promote it.

The "acculturation to assimilation" process leads to similar results in the same societies.[2] This process operates on three levels. First, there is acculturation—the shedding of foreign language, customs, work and leisure-time habits, and the adopting of new cultural traits. This is followed by a decrease in the social distance between the immigrant group and the other component groups of the society. Finally, feelings of belongingness and group identification change. Intermarriage may be viewed as part of the final stage of assimilation, a process which begins with conflict and competition and ends after an intermediate phase of accommodation.

The relatively low rate of intermarriage of Jews (random selection of mates by Jews from the general population would result in a 97 percent rate) is the result of resistance to this race-relations cycle. Jews are concentrated geographically, with about half of them residing in the New York City area, and more than another third in the next ten largest metropolitan centers. Furthermore, most Jews live in neighborhoods with sizable percentages of Jews. This cohesiveness is vitiated somewhat because the majority of young Jews attend college.[3]

Other inhibiting factors which operate against assimilation, the final step in the race-relations cycle, are Jewish education and Jewish self-consciousness, or identification with the Jewish group. Contrary to what might be expected, the decline in cultural differences has not been accompanied by a decline in Jewish self-consciousness. The heightened self-consciousness seems to be the result of the growth of Nazi anti-Semitism and the Nazi definition of Jew along racial and ancestral lines, reinforced by the more recent problems of Jews in Russia and the Middle East.[4] Unsettling, however, are the statistics of intermarriage in Washington, D.C., San Francisco and vicinity, Iowa, and Indiana, unless they are viewed only as regional aberrations of an overall lower rate (see table 1).[5] On the basis of interviews of members of approximately 7,550 households carried out between late 1970 and early 1972, however, they seem to be the first indications of the future overall rate.[22] On this basis, the efficacy of the survival formula of neighborhood and education must be seriously doubted.[23] There can be no doubt that the likelihood of intermarriage increases with increased acculturation; the Washington survey indicated that persons born in the United States, with an educational achievement beyond high school and with high professional status, are the most likely to enter into intermarriage.

TABLE 1
RATES OF INTERMARRIAGE

Source	Locale	Period	Number of Intermarriages per 100 Marriages
Engelman (6)	Germany	1901	14
	Germany	1906	17
	Germany	1911	22
	Germany	1916	42
	Germany	1921	25
	Germany	1927	35
	U.S.S.R.	1926	15
	Switzerland	1880	5.7
	Switzerland	1900	7
	Switzerland	1920	13
Barr & Cahnman (7)	Switzerland	1950	19.4
Davis (8)	Australia	1911	20.5
	Australia	1921	22.9
	Australia	1933	15.5
Rosenberg (9)	Canada	1926–30	2.5
	Canada	1931–35	2.6
	Canada	1936–40	3.2
	Canada	1941–45	5
	Canada	1946–50	4.8
	Canada	1951–55	6.2
	Canada	1956–60	7.6

TABLE 1—Continued
RATES OF INTERMARRIAGE

Source	Locale	Period	Number of Intermarriages per 100 Marriages
Davis (8)	United States	1776–1840	20.5
Glick (10)	United States	1957	7
Greeley (11)	United States	1961–68 (college graduates)	16
Lenn (12)	United States	1971	11
	United States	1971 (age 20–24)	33
Sklare (13)	New York City	1908–12	1.2
Kennedy (14)	New Haven	1870	0
	New Haven	1900	1.18
	New Haven	1930	2.99
	New Haven	1940	5.68
Shanks (15)	New Haven	1958	5
Kennedy (16)	Cincinnati	1916–19	3.6
	Stanford, Conn.	1938	7.2
Rosenthal (17)	New London, Conn.	1938	5.2
Goldstein &	Providence	1963 (parents)	4.5
Goldscheider (18)	Providence	1963 (men, 30 & under)	9
Rosenthal (17)	Dallas	1939	6.1
	Duluth	1939	15.1
Shanks (15)	Trenton	1937	1
	Des Moines	1949	8
Sklare (13)	Camden, N.J.	1964	4
	Boston	1965 (whole sample)	7
	Boston	1965 (30 & under)	20
Lazerwitz (19)	N. Illinois	1966–67	11
Shanks (15)	Indianapolis	1941	12
Rosenthal (20)	Indiana	1960–63	49
	Marion County, Ind.	1958	34.5
	San Francisco	1938	6.9
	San Francisco	1958	17.2
	Marin County, Calif.	1958	37
	Washington, D.C.	1956	13
	Iowa	1953–59	42
Massarik &	United States	1961–65	17.4
Chenkin (21)	United States	1966–72	31.7

NOTE: Parenthetical numbers in Source column refer to notes on pp. 156–57 below.

Researchers have identified numerous other factors which are related to the rate of intermarriage. Community size appears to be one of these.

In Iowa between 1953 and 1959, in towns of 10,000 or more, the rate fluctuated between 36.3 percent and 53.6 percent averaging 42.4 percent. It was almost twice as high in smaller towns and rural areas.[24] Similarly in Indiana: the intermarriage rate in the five counties with the highest concentration of Jews was 38.6 percent, while in the other eighty-two counties it was 63.5 percent.[25] However, because many communities have their own unique qualities, narrower generalizations are difficult to make. San Francisco is very cosmopolitan, while Washington, D.C., has a very transient and highly professionalized population, factors which apparently also seem to increase the rate of intermarriage.

A major concern is the fate of the children of intermarried couples. Morris Fishberg, in an early-twentieth-century study on New York, reported that 75 percent of all children born to Jews married to Christians are baptized at birth. The remaining 25 percent are reared as Jews.[26] In Washington, D.C., in 1956, 17.5 percent of the children of intermarried Jewish households were identified as Jews.[27] This contrasted with the experience in Providence. There, when the non-Jewish parent converted, all the children involved were reared as Jews, while when there was no conversion, 84 were reared as Jews and 60 were not, or a 58 percent rate.[28] The disparity between the Washington and Providence rates may be attributed to the former being a community with a transient population while the latter is an old, well-established Jewish community with a strong organizational structure.

The study of intermarriage rates also suffers from methodological problems. In Boston the average rate in 1965 was thought to be 7 percent, but this does not reflect the true situation since the rate varies from a low of 3 percent for husbands 51 years of age and over to a high of 20 percent for husbands age 30 and younger. Since the latter group is predominant in new marriage formations, the figure of 20 percent should be approximately the current rate.[29]

This conclusion is borne out by two other studies. In a 1971 survey of Reform Jews, the rate of intermarriage generally increased steadily as age decreased (see table 2). A comparable rate is seen in a 1968 survey of the marital status of college graduates of 1961 (see table 3). That losses to the Jewish group correlate with the rate of intermarriage is most apparent in the religious identity of the children of such unions. But it is exacerbated in other ways as well. Fewer women intermarry, perhaps half, than do men. The result is significant demographically in that, as

TABLE 2
PERCENTAGE INTERMARRIED BY AGE

Religion of spouse	Age						
	80+	70–79	60–69	50–59	40–49	30–39	20–29
Jewish	100	87	93	90	87	89	82
Non-Jewish	0	10	8	10	12	11	18

SOURCE: Lenn and associates, *Rabbi and Synagogue in Reform Judaism*, p. 218.

spinsters, unmarried women typically do not bear children. Furthermore, urban dwellers, professionals, white-collar workers, and the highly educated tend to have fewer children. Jews are concentrated in each of these categories. They are 96 percent urban. In addition, they are almost 7 years older than the average American (their median age is 36.6 years against 29.9 years). Jewish fertility, for all of these reasons, is only 75 percent that of Catholics and Protestants. Even where they share characteristics with other religious groups, their birth rate is lower: 14 percent lower than other urban groups and 5–15 percent lower than others in the professions and white-collar occupations.[30]

Intermarried Jewish couples also have smaller families, a higher percentage are childless, and there are fewer higher-order births than among couples born Jewish. Where the husband and wife were both born Jewish, 9.7 percent were childless, while 26.1 percent of the intermarried couples were childless. The mean number of children where both parents were born Jewish was 2.2; it was 1.6 where there was intermarriage.[31]

TABLE 3
INTERMARRIAGE AMONG COLLEGE GRADUATES (1968)

	Marital Status (percentage)			
	In-married	Out-married	Unmarried	No response
Men	62	16[a]	19	3
Women	71	6[b]	18	5

SOURCE: Greeley, Follow-up of *The Great Aspirations Study.*
[a] 18% of married respondents.
[b] 8% of married respondents.

Such figures and trends are perceived as a threat to the survival of Jews in the United States and other nations, with the exception of Israel. Although statistics are not as available outside of the United States, intermarriage rates are known to be high, sharing the same demographic problems as those of the Jews of America. No activity or pronouncement by laity or clergy has been successful in stemming intermarriage. Mordecai M. Noah declared in 1845 that if marriage between Jews and Christians were permitted, Judaism and Jews would disappear in two or three generations.[32] In the middle of the nineteenth century, congregations in New York City barred synagogue seats and cemetery rights to those who intermarried.[33] David Einhorn, a leading radical Reform rabbi, viewed each intermarriage as a nail in the coffin of Judaism.[34] The generally negative attitudes toward intermarriage on the part of Jewish parents seem ineffective.

Some researchers believe Jewish intermarriage to be quite low, considering the size of the Jewish group and intermarriage rates among other religious groups.[35] A study of a midwestern suburb indicated that virtually no Jews of Eastern European origin, in the first, second, and third generations, would be happy with intermarriage in their family. Only about one in five would be indifferent to it. There was less concern among those of German and mixed descent. Somewhat more than half of the fourth generation would feel indifferent or happy about their children's intermarriage. Relatively few oppose intermarriage out of concern for Jewish survival or because of Judaism (14 percent). Their primary concern was that it would lead to marital discord. Romantic love was viewed as more important than Jewishness: 85 percent preferred a loved gentile to an unloved Jew as a mate for their child. Only 1 percent would reject a child who might intermarry, while 94 percent would accept the marriage and retain a meaningful relationship with their child.[36]

The Jewish experience throughout history has always included intermarriage. Current trends in most Jewish communities lead to the conclusion that intermarriage will continue and in all probability increase. Attempts to stem this trend, increased Jewish education for the young, and other institutional programs will certainly not be completely effective. Therefore, it would seem that the Jews should turn once again to conversion as a historically tested Jewish survival mechanism. Bernard Lazerwitz states the case succinctly: "The basic threat to Jewish continuity does not stem from intermarriage. Rather, intermarriage (without conversion) is but a symptom of diaspora Jewry's growing dissatisfaction with contemporary Jewish institutions and cultural forms." [37] Similarly, the Levinsons write:

> Whether the rate of intermarriage by Jews rises or falls in the future will depend not on pronouncements for or against intermarriage as such, but on more fundamental social and psychological changes: in secularization and urbanization of American society, in the bases that can be found for building a distinctive but not insular Jewish identity, in the emotional quality of the Jewish family and the like. [38]

Until these monumental changes in Jewish life come about—and it is doubtful if even they can stem the tide of intermarriage—conversion may help maintain the Jewish body politic.

Furthermore, each instance of intermarriage may also have a multiplier effect. The multiplier effect comes about when intermarriage attains such frequency that it creates greater approval for itself. It becomes fashionable and acceptable. [39]

Rather than being viewed solely as a threat to Jewish survival, intermarriage may be considered an opportunity to increase the number of Jews. If an equal number of Jewish men and women intermarried and then succeeded in maintaining their own Jewishness and inducing their spouses to identify with their group, the Jewish community would be magnified rather than diminished by intermarriage. [40] The problem is to welcome the prospective convert and to provide something worth converting to.

CONVERSION

As we have shown, Judaism developed an anti-conversionist stance in the centuries after the establishment of Christianity and Islam. Jewish attitudes on conversion have been mixed. There have been few individual advocates of conversion, and still fewer organizations have made it their central cause or even a cause of much importance. On the other hand, there have been many outspoken opponents of proselyting. For the most part, however, most Jews have been and remain indifferent to conversion.

Typical of those who oppose conversion to Judaism was Rabbi Akiba Egger the younger, of Posen in Prussian Poland, who in 1834 promulgated a decree in which he instructed an inquirer to abide by the Prussian law which forbade Jews to accept converts.[41]

Nathan Adler, the chief rabbi of the British Empire, sent a number of letters to religious and lay leaders in Australia in the 1870s to prohibit all proselytization except in cases that he specifically approved. In a letter addressed to the president and members of the Jewish congregation of Geelong, Victoria, he wrote as follows on November 3, 1874:

> It is known to you that the local Beth Din is not allowed to allow proselytes without my direct sanction. And it is also known to you that in principle I am very much opposed to making Jewish proselytes and since thirty years that I hold office I have opposed with all my powers the marriages out of our pale.[42]

In 1928 in Argentina, on the initiative of Rabbi Shaul Sithon of the Syrian Jewish community and with the approval of the Ashkenazic rabbis, a decision was made to accept no conversions. This prohibition was supported by the chief rabbi of Palestine, A. I. Kook. It is still maintained by the Orthodox of Argentina.[43]

At a symposium held in Israel in 1956, entitled "Should Jews Missionize Christians and Muslims?", Rabbi J. L. Meirman and Benjamin Mazur stated that the establishment of missions is contrary to the spirit of Judaism. In addition, they felt, such efforts would be considered competitive by other religious groups and therefore harmful. Finally, they indicated that ready acceptance of proselytes would disturb the integrity of the Jewish religious way of life. Others, among them Rabbi S. I. Zeivin and Joseph Klausner, disagreed, feeling that national solutions to these problems would evolve.[44]

A leading nineteenth-century Reform rabbi, David Einhorn of Baltimore, included in his prayerbook a service for the acceptance of proselytes.[45] Rabbi Adolph Moses, in a sermon delivered at the Hebrew Union College in Cincinnati in 1894, suggested that the name "Judaism," which he felt was a nationalist term, be replaced by the universalist "Yahvism." He was convinced of the existence of large numbers of prospective converts and maintained that the name change would make the religion more acceptable to them.[46] In response to a petition by a non-Jew to Rabbi Henry Berkowitz of Kansas City in 1890, two leaders of Reform Judaism, Isaac M. Wise and Kaufmann Kohler, indicated that circumcision was not essential for conversion.[47] Circumcision is still not required by Reform Judaism. It is by Conservative and Orthodox Judaism, but where necessitated by reasons of health, a symbolic circumcision is sufficient.

The Reform Central Conference of American Rabbis, while never hostile to conversion, has taken only minimal steps to encourage active proselyting. In 1927 it published a manual for instructing converts. In 1950 an effort to do something more led to the creation of a committee to study practical means "of extending the influence and acceptance of the Jewish religion." During the next year a committee on the unaffiliated was appointed. After six years of study and the acceptance of its report, a call was made for the preparation of literature, radio and television programs, and congregational preaching missions. Nothing came of this proposal.[48] Even now little has changed among Reform rabbis. Only 8 percent feel "strongly," and 25 percent agree "somewhat," that more time and energy should be given in making an effort to win converts.[49] Orthodox and Conservative rabbis would resist efforts to recruit proselytes even more than Reform rabbis.

Israelis, in a survey made in 1964–65, were generally negative toward seeking converts. Seventy-six percent of the parents and 70 percent of students surveyed opposed such conversion abroad, while 73 percent of the parents and 68 percent of students opposed it in Israel.[50]

Acceptance of converts by Jews is often mixed. Startlingly, some converts are identified as gentiles. This may simply indicate incomplete assimilation into the Jewish group. But it also reflects the remarkable influence of ethnicity among Jews, in spite of an extremely high level of acculturation. In some instances, however, converts to Judaism are characterized "as more Jewish than anyone else." This indicates the feeling that such converts have not only become acculturated to Jewish ways but have also been detached from gentile clique groups.[51]

Formal institutional efforts to develop modern Jewish missionary activities have been few and of minimal effectiveness. In the late nineteenth century a British attorney, John Oswald Simon, proposed a "church of Israel" for gentiles who need and want the Jewish system of theology and moral teachings without the associated cultic elements. He was convinced that many Christians were alienated from their own theology but could identify with the Jewish view of God. He also felt that many Christians could no longer accept the teaching of the vicarious atonement for sin through Jesus. His proposal grew out of a conviction that Judaism would help non-Jews and that Jews had an obligation to engage in such an activity. Jewish ritual practices, such as circumcision, the eating of unleavened bread during Passover, dietary laws, and Sabbath on the seventh day, were viewed as sacred but not essential for those "who were not hereditary members of the House of Israel." [52]

Three years later, writing in a popular secular journal, Simon continued his plea for a Jewish mission to gentiles. He declared that Judaism's mission was the achievement of a universal religious brotherhood. The purpose of Jewish separatism, he said, was to preserve Jewish identity so that Judaism could fulfill this goal. Neither Christianity nor Islam was of equal value with Judaism. The Jewish mission was especially necessary at the time, Simon felt, because a wave of agnosticism was sweeping England. He called for a special Judaism for gentiles "free from the restraint of that orientalism which in the ordinary Jewish place of worship is justifiably preserved." [53]

The next year a number of prominent English lay and religious leaders, both Jewish and gentile, responded to Simon's proposal. Some saw it as a fulfillment of the Jewish mission, but others raised the same objections that are still used against such schemes. A specific Sunday service geared for Christians, they said, would weaken Judaism for Jews. Efforts spent in bringing gentiles to Judaism could be better spent in making Jews adhere to their faith. Such a program would also promote anti-Semitism by challenging the dominant faith.[54] In any event, after this series of articles and the lively exchange it engendered, nothing concrete seems to have taken place.

The first Jewish missionary society of modern times was organized by David Horowitz, a Swedish-born American journalist. Horowitz had an Orthodox Jewish background and was married to a convert. In 1944 he incorporated the United Israel World Union, "an international movement to disseminate the decalogue both within and beyond the confines of Jewry." He gained little support from either rabbis or Jewish laymen, apparently because of the kind of Judaism he advocated. He called for a reunion of "the two separated houses of Israel whose breech has remained unhealed since the split of the Commonwealth after Solomon's reign." Proselytes of this movement established their own congregations in Wilbur, West Virginia, and West Olive, Michigan.[55]

In 1955 or 1956 the World Union for the Propagation of Judaism was established in Israel by Dr. Israel Ben-Zeev, the head of Arab schools in Israel and a professor at Bar-Ilan University. This movement elicited little response.[56] Presumably, converting the Arabs of Israel to Judaism would solve the problem of a significant non-Jewish minority in a Jewish state, in the same way that a similar problem was resolved in ancient Israel.

In 1958 Robert Gordis, a leading American Conservative rabbi, issued a call for a conference of national Jewish religious organizations and rabbis to discuss all aspects of Jewish missionary activities. He specifically suggested the establishment of a pilot missionary effort in Japan, where there seemed to be great interest in Judaism and where the small number of Christians would not complicate interfaith relations. He advocated information centers for the United States. His call for missionary activities was motivated by the need to compensate for the Jews lost during World War II and those being "spiritually asphyxiated under communism," as well as the benefits which Judaism offered gentiles theologically and in family and personal relations.[57]

In 1959, in response to the Israeli conversionist group and with promised rabbinical support, Ben Maccabee, a refugee from Nazi Germany and a Chicago engineer, led an effort to organize the Jewish Information Society. He was supported by many prominent Reform and Conservative rabbis and laymen. The society published a monthly journal from 1960 until 1969. It included articles explaining aspects of Judaism and testimonials from converts to Judaism.[58] The Jewish Information Society was clearly conversionist in purpose and was the most sustained and broadly based effort to win converts to Judaism in modern times, but like all such efforts, it floundered because of general lack of interest among Jews. In a personal communication, Maccabee writes that "promises of financial and literary contributions were reneged. . . . I am sorry to report that there are not even ten dedicated persons or foundations willing to make substantial contributions to the cause. . . . I nevertheless persisted spending thirteen years and substantial funds until illness stopped me."

In 1949, Leo Baeck, the leading liberal rabbi of Germany before and during World War II, spoke of the mission of Israel.

Mankind is hungry and thirsts for that which Judaism can say, what Jews full of Judaism can say. Many an example can be remembered. Judaism became, so to speak, attractive to the gentiles and many a one became a proselyte, educated people, high-minded people. Should we not begin anew? Should we not send our missionaries to Asia, to East Asia and to other places to the people there waiting for us? We are in need of expansion for our own sake.[59]

This most eloquent plea brought only a "confused, evasive and unimaginative" response.[60] Allen S. Maller, a Reform rabbi committed to this mission, sees it as the Jewish "obligation to teach all men and to welcome them into the Jewish people. . . . There can be no reason to prefer an assimilated Jew who has no desire to be Jewish to an interested gentile unless one believes in racial theories for either Jews or gentiles."[61] Rabbi Maller has organized a group known as JOIN US (Jews United to Welcome Christians into the Family of ISRAEL).[62]

The absence of a central Jewish secular or religious organization, and generally inadequate statistical record-keeping by the numerous national Jewish organizations of all kinds in this area, make an estimate of the number of converts to Judaism most tenuous. David Max Eichhorn, a Reform rabbi who has maintained a zealous interest in the subject for several decades, provides the most detailed data. In 1954 he estimated that Reform rabbis converted between 1,000 and 1,200 persons per year and Conservative rabbis between 500 and 550. At this time 333 members of the Central Conference of American Rabbis indicated that they had converted 855 men and 3,390 women during their ministries. Another 120 members estimated their conversions at 1,193 men and 4,106 women. By calculating the number of rabbis, 453, with the number of conversions, 9,544, and their years in the rabbinate, 7,744, Eichhorn found that the rate of conversion was 1.2 per year per rabbi.[63] Rabbi Leon Fram of Detroit reported 27 conversions during 1952–53, and Rabbi Morris Goldstein of San Francisco specified 125 for the five-year period 1948–53.[64] Eichhorn estimated in 1963 that between 2,000 and 3,000 non-Jews were converting annually.[65]

Maller estimated in 1967 that 7,000 converts were coming into Judaism annually. He felt that by 1980 there would be more than 100,000 families in which one parent was a convert. This would be 10 percent of the families formed in a fifteen-year period.[66]

It may be assumed that the conversion rate is much higher now, what with the growing number of intermarriages and of rabbinically sponsored conversion classes. In addition, the rate of conversion seems to rise among younger Jews. In a Providence study of 1963, the rate of conversion of wives of Jewish males 60 years and over was 0 percent. The rate of those 59 years and younger varied between 33.3 percent and 100 percent.[67] This is borne out further in a 1971 survey indicating that while one in three Reform Jews of the sample aged 20–24 intermarry, three out of four of their spouses convert to Judaism.[68] In the National Jewish Population Study, it was discovered that about one-fourth of all intermarrying non-Jewish females converted while few of the non-Jewish males converted. However, nearly half of both sexes who were non-Jewish prior to marriage identified as Jewish, regardless of formal conversion.[69]

Between 1948 and 1968, 2,288 proselytes were accepted by the religious courts of Israel out of a total of 4,010 applicants. Beginning with 1970 greater leniency was exhibited due to both the increased immigration from Russia, where intermarriage is prevalent, and the amended Law of Return. In 1971 the Ministry of Religious Affairs established schools for prospective proselytes.[70]

Throughout Jewish history many converts, perhaps most of them, converted because of marriage to a Jew. Some, including those who strongly favor conversion, estimate that 90 to 95 percent come to Judaism because of marriage.[71] This practice, however, has been generally condemned as resulting in insincere conversions and conversions of convenience rather than from conviction.

Richard Rubenstein strongly disagrees with this view. First of all, he contends, the desire to have a religiously unified home is a healthy reason for conversion. In addition, he maintains, gentiles often consciously seek to become Jewish, or may even unconsciously want to identify with Jews, and marriage to a Jewish mate provides a socially accepted motive for conversion. He writes: ". . . marriage is the best rather than the worst reason for conversion today. Young people create the first atom of community life by forming a family. They share each other's fate and destiny. It is best that this explicitly be shared within a common religio-ethnic community."[72]

The following is at least a partial profile of the background characteristics of converts and those who marry them.[73] The typical convert is a non-Jewish woman married to a Jewish man. (Conservative rabbis report one male convert to every six female converts; Reform rabbis, one male to every four females.)[74] Families with Jewish converts are of distinctly higher social status than other Jewish change groups. Spouses of converts report a greater amount of Jewish education than those whose wives do not convert. The spouses of converts are also active in Jewish religious and organizational life. Those who intermarry without conversion are frequently marginal religio-ethnic members marrying similar persons. They have less religious training and education than most of their faith. After marriage such persons frequently reduce or eliminate any involvement in their childhood faith.

The faithfulness of converts has been attested to. In his 1954 survey of 785 Reform and Conservative rabbis, Eichhorn discovered that a majority of the rabbis ranked Jewish-born and converted members of their congregations about equal in their Jewish loyalties and interests, but they also tended to describe converts as more loyal more frequently than they accorded this designation to the Jewish-born.[75] For this reason, Eichhorn views converts as a precious spiritual asset and a challenge to the Jewish-born to be more worthy of their priceless spiritual inheritance.

This accords well with the Lazerwitz and Lenn studies. Lazerwitz found that converts usually blended successfully into their new religio-ethnic community and were often more active than persons born Jewish.[76] Utilizing a Religiosity Index including belief in God, Jewish identification, ethical living, and other such factors, Lenn found that Reform Jews with two Jewish parents ranked 47 percent on the scale against 77 percent for those with one non-Jewish parent. Reform Jews married to converts are more religious than those married to born Jews, while those married to spouses who have not converted are still more religious. Furthermore, those who intermarry and remain Jewish tend to be more religious ritualistically than those whose spouses are born Jews.[77]

A number of non-Jewish groups have converted to Judaism in recent decades. Under the leadership of Donato Manduzio, a winegrower living in the small town of San Nicandro in southern Italy, twenty-three peasant families adopted Judaism. About 1930, inspired by a dream, Manduzio began to preach the truth of Judaism and the necessity of conversion to it. In spite of threats by the local clergy, the hostility of the Fascist authorities, and discouragement by the rabbinate of Rome, he and his group persisted. Their conversion was recognized in 1944. Manduzio died in 1948. His followers migrated to Israel in

1949, where they dissolved as a group.[78] A recent study of this group (1973) found that they numbered about one hundred people, were well integrated into Israeli society, and that "their marginality as one-time gentiles has given way to their normalcy as Jews and Israelis." [79]

There are records of individual blacks professing Judaism in the antebellum South of the United States. Most of the small urban black Jewish sects that originated after World War I attached themselves to charismatic figures. They originated primarily in the West Indies and established independent congregations in a few American cities. Their Judaism is seen as a social device to separate them from lower-status southern Negroes and to provide a way to identify with a successful white community. This is more plausible since Jews more than other whites have also been a marginal people who have suffered discrimination. The claim of these blacks to have recovered a lost religion and national identity may also have been an attempt to develop a unique culture of their own. The black Jewish sects were frequently syncretistic. The major groups are the Bnei Israel, the Commandment Keepers, the Temple of the Gospel of the Kingdom, and the Kohel Beth B'nai Yisrael —all told numbering between 2,000 and 6,000 members. Relations with the white Jewish community are most tenuous. After World War II small numbers converted, attaching themselves to established congregations.[80] Deteriorating relations between Jews and blacks and growing black ethnicity and racial pride probably preclude any sizable conversion to Judaism.

In 1967 a group of about seventy American black self-proclaimed Jews, chiefly from Chicago, migrated to Liberia. After considerable difficulties there, they left for Israel in 1969. Because their credentials as Jews were not clear, they were not accepted under the Law of Return. A number of factors led to considerable tension between them and the Israeli government and other Israelis. They proclaimed that the Jews were originally black and that the other Jews of Israel were not of the "seed of Abraham." They agitated because of difficulties in living conditions and in gaining employment. There were also difficulties within the group, resulting in one dissident being killed. In 1971 the Israeli government resolved to get rid of them by not renewing their visas. Robert Weisbrod concludes that "they are...black nationalist zealots who have been victimized by their own zealotry which rendered them unassimilable and unacceptable in a Jewish state." [81]

In Uganda, in the 1920s, the Boyudaya, a Jewish society, was formed by a politico-military leader named Semei Kakungulu. Numbering about 500 people, it is recognized by the Uganda government as a religious community under the name "The Propagation of Judaism in Uganda—Moses Synagogue." [82]

Judaizers, persons who follow the Jewish religion in whole or in part and claim to be Jews, have a long history in Russia, apparently going back to the fifteenth century. The Judaizers seem to have included converts as well as persons who shared some Jewish beliefs and practices. After an absence, they reappeared at the beginning of the eighteenth century, although there is no proof of a link to the earlier group. Their acceptance of Judaism seems chiefly to relate to a profound study of the Bible. The most prominent such sect was the Molokan, founded by Simeon Uklein, noted for his biblical erudition. His disciple, Sundiekoo, called for greater association with Jews. Officials set their number at 3,770 in 1823, but there may have been as many as 20,000. They were systematically persecuted and kept away from Jews, with some exiled to Siberia and inducted into the army. All discrimination was abolished in 1905. The Molokan observed circumcision, the Sabbath, and the dietary laws, and covered their heads. They tried to mingle with Jews and marry with them. Some migrated to Israel, where they were completely integrated into the general society. [83]

A small village located sixty miles from Mexico City claims to be Jewish. The inhabitants have a slight knowledge of Hebrew. They seem to share many characteristics with the Iglesiade Dios, the Latin American version of the Protestant Church of God. [84]

The integrity of Jewish communities in the diaspora, potentially even in Israel, is threatened by diminished relative and absolute numbers. Attrition is brought about by increasing intermarriage, frequently without conversion, and therefore losses from Judaism, low fertility rates, strong pressures for acculturation and absorption into the general culture, freely in some countries and forced in others, together with a general malaise about Judaism and Jewish culture and affairs. In Israel many Jews identify more as Israeli nationals than as members of a religious group. There is also the problem of the large numbers of Arabs both in Israel and the occupied territories, who threaten to overwhelm the Jews because of their very high birth rate.

The process of acculturation is thwarted somewhat where institutional and cultural life is strong. Events and developments such as the Holocaust, Arab threats to Israel, anti-Semitism in one place and another, and the rise of ethnicity, especially in America, have helped to reinforce Jewish identity.

At the same time, many of the special benefits that accrued to Jews, because they were Jews, are gone. Economic specialization is far less important than it was, since economic systems have become more open, inducing utilization of the best person for a particular economic role regardless of any other characteristic. Additionally, Jews are no longer favored by some ruling elites as buffers between themselves and the dominated classes of their societies.

Theological belief seems to be less important to more and more Jews. The Reconstructionist movement rejects the ideology of a chosen people and a Jewish mission. Jews generally continue to see themselves as a special, separate group, almost a super-tribe, dispersed throughout the world but still bound together by ties of lineage, history, and destiny.

All these factors, together with the general Jewish malaise about seeking converts, even among those who marry Jews, makes it difficult to see where Jewries will gain the persons they need to maintain their present numbers, let alone grow numerically. Major, well-organized missionary efforts seem a remote possibility. It is equally unlikely that Jewish communities and congregations will be given quotas as were those of Babylonia more than a millennium ago.

Conclusion

EVERY individual develops his personality in response to his physical, psychological, and social milieu. With this "persona" he copes with his environment in the most effective way he can. The success of his confrontation with society may be measured by whether he survives and by the quality of his life and satisfactions.

A similar process is operative for conglomerates of individuals, whether in small or large groupings. Each group develops its own particular nature or character as part of its response to its environment. When a group survives over a long period of time, this is indicative of its success in adjusting to repeated changes while maintaining its identity. Frequently, the content is altered in the process, but the identity remains. Those nations and peoples who have become a part of history were unable to meet the challenges of their changing milieu. Because the character of a people cannot change radically or quickly, broad social changes may come too late and the right options may not be available at the right time. It is not surprising that many peoples do not survive.

Among those peoples who have survived are the Jews, whose social framework, Judaism, has a history of approximately 3,200 years. Its survival through the millennia depended on its ability to adapt to numerous changes. The most dramatic changes were those from nomadism to settled life after the conquest of Canaan. Another radical change was the development of a national state with its special problems, followed by the dissolution of the state, which spread the former inhabitants over vast distances, where they lived as enclaves. In this latter stage several serious difficulties were faced. First, the people had to find a way to live among more sophisticated and advanced cultures, borrowing from them while maintaining their own identity. This was managed with great effectiveness. Second, they had to survive occasional periods of prolonged hostility and violence. This too was effected, but at the cost of considerable numbers of adherents. Proselyting was one of the tools utilized by the Jews not only to assimilate conquered peoples in the biblical and Hasmonean periods but to replenish and even enlarge their ranks at other times. Viewed in this perspective, the Jewish attitude on proselyting becomes one of the key factors in understanding Judaism. The problems of the Jews in any period may be better understood through a knowledge of contemporary Jewish attitudes on proselyting. In this way proselyting activities may serve as an indication for determining the social role of Judaism and Jews in any given situation.

Conversion to Judaism served the survival needs of the Jewish group throughout its history. While official and popular attitudes on proselyting occasionally were out of harmony with actual practice, ideology usually caught up with the practices demanded by necessity. When peoples do not survive, it is clear that they responded inadequately or not at all to the challenges facing them. Just the opposite is the case when they do survive. Conversion was one of the major survival tools invented and repeatedly used by Jews.

In its earliest period conversion served to assimilate relatively large numbers of conquered peoples into the national-religious entity of the conquerors. Even though the invading Hebrews adopted many of the religious practices of the Canaanites, they integrated them within the Jewish framework and identity system. In this way a small group of invading tribes became a national entity. The same pattern was followed almost a millennium later, during the Second Jewish Commonwealth under the Hasmoneans. Again conquered peoples had the opportunity of joining themselves to the conquerors through conversion.

This was the last time, until the establishment of the State of Israel, that Jews would have the opportunity for mass proselyting, although conversion continued to be encouraged and practiced under different but equally pressing circumstances. No longer a tool to manage conquered peoples, conversion was practiced to compensate for losses suffered in war and through Jews themselves joining other cults and philosophies. Proselyting was also defensive since there was considerable competition for the adherence of the peoples of the Greco-Roman world. It was also a way of extending Jewish influence both socially and commercially. The practice of conversion was reinforced by tradition and ideology, both in the Bible, with its emphasis on the Jewish mission, and in the writings of the rabbis, who generally supported the biblical message.

During such periods as the time of Ezra and Nehemiah and following the establishment of Christianity and Islam, a changed attitude toward proselyting was necessitated by changed conditions. The key once again was not ideology but survival. Ideology was often twisted to meet the exigencies of specific conditions and the demands of survival. Physical survival and economic well-being came before pursuit of the tradition of proselyting, which itself was a survival mechanism.

Similarly, when large groups of gentiles converted to Judaism, they did so for their own survival needs. The Khazars, Yemenites, and Falashas apparently converted to maintain their national integrity. National expansion may have been behind the conversion of the ruling family of Adiabene. The Berbers of North Africa may have joined Judaism to raise their cultural level. Many other peoples throughout history, but particularly during the time of the Roman Empire, were seeking a more satisfying spiritual philosophy than the others available to them. The Jewish proselyting drive made such conversions possible, but only the special needs of the groups involved made the conversions take place.

While there is no doubt that conversions to Judaism occurred from the very earliest stage in the history of the Jews, a number of these were not recorded in the Jewish literature of the time. This was the case, except for a stray reference or two, with the Khazars and the Falashas. Yet there is no doubt that conversions took place among the Khazars and the Ethiopians. After a few centuries there was considerable interest in the Khazar conversion, probably as part of the campaign of Rabbinic Judaism against the sectarian Karaites.

It may have been felt that many of these national or large-group conversions took place for completely opportunistic reasons, and that while individuals who convert for such reasons are to be accepted, large corporate groups may not. Furthermore, the Judaism practiced by such converts may have been alien to that of the Jewish establishment. In the same way, large groups with their own traditions may have been unwilling, and even unable, to take on all the elements included in Judaism, for some aspects of the Jewish life-style may have been culturally alien to them even though the religion per se was perfectly acceptable. It would also have been difficult for a viable national group such as the Khazars or the Yemenites to place itself under the authority of rabbinical councils several hundred miles distant. Not only would the authority be unacceptable but intolerable taxation was also involved. Thus the independence of such converts could have led the mainstream of Judaism to ignore them rather than directly challenge or attempt to discipline them. Such efforts would probably have been in vain, in any event, and might have precipitated further difficulties.

It is also possible that large group conversions took place far from the centers of organized Jewish life, by peoples who left no literary remains. This is a possible explanation for the strong tradition that a number of Berber tribes in North Africa converted to Judaism, a subject discussed in Muslim historical works. It is not unlikely that a relatively small group of Jews in North Africa were swamped by large numbers of enthusiastic Berber converts, who neither maintained contact with the major Jewish center several thousand miles distant nor recorded the event, since they had no literature of their own. The strong oral and written traditions of such pre-Muslim conversions in both North Africa and Yemen are not corroborated in Jewish sources. This lack or omission is compensated by Muslim and Christian sources as well as by modern biological research.

The strong Jewish policy and attitude favoring proselyting goes back to the origins of Judaism and changed only gradually, and then never completely. The change was enough to lead most Jews and gentiles to believe that Judaism did not seek converts but only accepted them under special circumstances after putting many barriers before them. This change in both policy and attitude came about slowly because of the strong counter-mood. Reversion to the earlier view, which is made possible by altered conditions, has proven equally difficult. Legal barriers no longer prohibit Jews from seeking and winning converts. Church authorities have lost power everywhere. Some anti-conversionist pressure exists, but the greater social pressure comes from the anti-proselyte ideology, a development of the Middle Ages. Just as it took centuries for the original ideology to change, so it apparently will take a considerable period for the return to the original attitude that modern conditions now make possible.

Such a return has occurred gradually, however, at different times and in different places. Where the medieval system broke down and religious institutions lost their power before the onslaught of secular forces, Jews experienced greater freedom in all spheres of activity. Religion was given a subservient role first in Western Europe. The state became the primary social institution, with religious institutions serving the interests of the state. This social and political change was accompanied by the intellectual revolution of the Enlightenment, which furthered secularization. While individuals and groups gained greater freedom in religious matters, a fact reflected in the growth of sects and denominations, religion itself gradually counted for less in the hierarchy of human concerns. Increasingly, science, technology, commerce, secular literature, sociology, and politics replaced religion as areas of concern and as disciplines for the guidance and control of individual lives and society. Just at the time when Judaism has been freed from the shackles of the Middle Ages, it finds itself inhibited by the restrictive ideology of the time and thwarted by the general lack of concern for religious institutions and ideas. Now that it is once again possible to embark on campaigns for conversions and to be more open to individuals intent on conversion, the whole realm of religion and of conversion from one or no religion to another is of little concrete importance.

Yet there may be a special role for Judaism in the West, where the secular religions of scientism, nationalism, communism, as well as others, have not been complete successes. Great numbers of people feel a lack in their lives which they vaguely describe as spiritual. Religions based on man's depravity and on mythic salvation schemes do not seem to contain an answer to such cravings. Judaism, however, particularly where it expresses its belief in man's potential and fosters his fulfillment both sensuously and intellectually, may provide such an answer. To accomplish this Judaism must take a few steps forward from the closed medievalism it still retains, and which produces its enclavist and ghetto outlook on life, and several steps backward to those ancient attitudes which were outward-looking in their encouragement for seeking and winning converts.

Notes

CHAPTER 1

1. Martin Noth, *The History of Israel* (London, 1958), p. 3.
2. Ibid., p. 119.
3. Ibid., p. 69.
4. Ibid., p. 165; cf. pp. 2, 68 f., 119.
5. Louis Finkelstein, ed., *The Jews: Their History, Culture, and Religion* (New York, 1949), vol. 1, p. 17; Norman Gottwald, *A Light to the Nations* (New York, 1959), pp. 157–66.
6. Johannes Pedersen, *Israel: Its Life and Culture*, 1–11 (London, 1926), p. 15.
7. Ibid., p. 16.
8. Ibid., p. 40.
9. Ibid.; cf. pp. 13 ff., 22–43.
10. John Bright, *A History of Israel* (Philadelphia, 1959), p. 125.
11. Ibid., pp. 120–42.
12. John Bright, *Early Israel in Recent History Writing* (London, 1965), p. 114.
13. Yehezkel Kaufmann, *The Religion of Israel* (Chicago, 1960), p. 245.
14. Ibid., pp. 245–54; *The Biblical Account of the Conquest of Palestine* (Jerusalem, 1953), pp. 46–54, 91.
15. I. Engnell, *Gamla Testamentet. En Traditionshistorisk inledning* (Uppsala and Stockholm, 1945), vol. 1, p. 136. Cited in G. W. Anderson, "Some Aspects of the Uppsala School of Old Testament Study," *Harvard Theological Review* 43 (1950): 250.
16. Bright, *Early Israel in Recent History Writing*, p. 32.
17. Harry Orlinsky, "Old Testament Studies," in *Religion*, ed. Paul Ramsey (Englewood Cliffs, N.J., 1965), p. 82.
18. Ibid.
19. Ibid., p. 83.
20. George E. Mendenhall, "Biblical History in Transition," in *The Bible and the Ancient Near East*, ed. G. Ernest Wright (New York, 1961), p. 43.

147

CHAPTER 2

1. M. I. Rostovtzeff, *The Social and Economic History of the Hellenistic World* (Oxford, 1941), vol. 2, p. 1140.
2. C. C. McCown, "The Density of Population in Ancient Palestine," *Journal of Biblical Literature* 66 (1947): p. 427.
3. Ibid., p. 436.
4. Roland de Vaux, *Ancient Israel* (New York, 1965), p. 65.

CHAPTER 3

1. Pedersen, *Israel,* 1–11, p. 40.
2. Ibid., 111–IV.
3. T. J. Meek, "The Translation of *Ger* in the Hexateuch and Its Bearing on the Documentary Theory," *Journal of Biblical Literature* 64 (1930): 174. Much of this section is based on this article, pp. 172–80.
4. Max Weber, *Ancient Judaism* (Glencoe, Ill., 1952), pp. 336, 363.
5. Ibid., p. 150.
6. Louis Finkelstein, *The Pharisees: The Sociological Background of their Faith* (Philadelphia, 1946), vol. 2, p. 461.
7. Ibid., p. 516; cf. pp. 555–58.
8. Ibid., p. 556.
9. Pedersen, *Israel* 1-11, pp. 54, 455.
10. Bernard Bamberger, *Proselytism in the Talmudic Period,* rev. ed. (New York, 1968), pp. 80 f., 116, n. 82.
11. Solomon Zeitlin, "The Offspring of Intermarriage," *Jewish Quarterly Review* 51 (1960–61): 135.
12. Ibid., p. 138.
13. Ibid., p. 139.
14. Bamberger, *Proselytism in the Talmudic Period,* p. 16.
15. Ibid.
16. Ibid.

CHAPTER 4

1. For a fuller account of this motif, see H. H. Rowley's *Israel's Mission* (London, 1939) and *The Missionary Message of Israel* (London, 1945).
2. Weber, *Ancient Judaism,* pp. 362 ff.
3. Harry M. Orlinsky and Norman H. Snaith, *Studies on the Second Part of the Book of Isaiah* (Leiden, 1967), p. 48.
4. Ibid., p. 99.

CHAPTER 5

1. Mark Wischnitzer, *A History of Jewish Crafts and Guilds* (New York, 1965), pp. 15 ff.

2. Salo W. Baron, *A Social and Religious History of the Jews* (New York, 1952), vol. 1, p. 170.

3. Ibid., p. 171.

4. Joseph Klausner, *From Jesus to Paul* (London, 1946), pp. 32 ff.

5. Karl Kautsky, *Foundations of Christianity* (London, 1925), pp. 358 f.

CHAPTER 6

1. George Foot Moore, *Judaism* (Cambridge, Mass., 1932), vol. 1, p. 342.

2. Bamberger, *Proselytism in the Talmudic Period,* p. 169.

3. C. G. Montefiore and H. Loewe, *A Rabbinic Anthology* (London, 1938), p. 114.

4. Ibid., p. 568.

5. Ibid., p. 572.

6. Ibid., p. 574.

7. Ibid., p. 577; cf. Moore, *Judaism,* vol. 1, pp. 337, 348.

8. William G. Braude, *Jewish Proselyting* (Providence, R.I., 1940), p. 126.

9. Moore, *Judaism,* vol. 1, p. 323.

10. Ibid., p. 324.

11. Braude, *Jewish Proselyting,* p. 19.

12. Bamberger, *Proselytism in the Talmudic Period,* p. 274.

13. Ibid.

14. Braude, *Jewish Proselyting,* p. 8.

15. Moore, *Judaism,* vol. 1, p. 335.

16. Joseph Klausner, *The Messianic Idea in Israel* (New York, 1955), p. 473.

17. Ibid., p. 478.

18. Ibid.

19. Ibid., p. 479.

20. Ibid.

21. Ibid., p. 482.

22. Solomon Zeitlin, *The Rise and Fall of the Judean State* (Philadelphia, 1962), vol. 1, p. 17.

23. Ibid., p. 32.

24. Bamberger, *Proselytism in the Talmudic Period,* pp. 102 f., 296 f.

25. Ibid., p. 63.

26. Louis M. Epstein, *Marriage Laws in the Bible and the Talmud* (Cambridge, Mass., 1942), p. 153. The rest of this paragraph is based on material in this volume.

27. Lou H. Silberman, "Reproduction, Prohibition, and Invalidity: An Examination of the Halachic Development Concerning Intermarriage," *CCAR Journal* 15 (1968): 3–8; Maurice Samuel, *Race, Nation and People in the Jewish Bible* (Syracuse, 1967), pp. 13 f., 26.

28. Karl Kautsky, *Are the Jews a Race?* (London, 1926), pp. 114 f.

29. Weber, *Ancient Judaism,* p. 336.

30. Ibid., pp. xxiii ff., 337 ff., 354.

CHAPTER 7

1. Kaufmann Kohler, *Jewish Theology* (New York, 1928), p. 412.
2. John Peterson, *Missionary Methods of Judaism in the Early Roman Empire* (Chicago, 1946), pp. 161 ff.
3. Erwin R. Goodenough, "Philo's Exposition of the Law and His *De Vita Mosis*," *Harvard Theological Review* 26 (1933): 113.
4. Ibid., p. 109.
5. Ibid., p. 114.
6. Ibid., p. 124.

CHAPTER 8

1. Moore, *Judaism*, vol. 1, pp. 338–42.
2. Solomon Zeitlin, "Proselytes and Proselytism During the Second Commonwealth and the Early Tannaitic Period," *Harry Austryn Wolfson Jubilee Volume*, (Jerusalem, 1956), vol. 2, p. 881.
3. Klausner, *From Jesus to Paul*, p. 43.
4. Zeitlin, "Proselytes and Proselytism," p. 881.
5. Ibid.
6. Solomon Zeitlin, "Beginnings of Christianity and Judaism," *Jewish Quarterly Review*, 27 (1936–37): 389.
7. Harry A. Wolfson, *Philo* (Cambridge, Mass., 1948), vol. 2, p. 369.
8. Ralph Marcus, "The *Sebomenoi* in Josephus," *Jewish Social Studies* 14 (1952): 247.
9. Wolfson, *Philo*, vol. 2, pp. 369–74, 417; vol. 1, p. 179.
10. Solomon Zeitlin, "Who Is a Jew?" *Jewish Quarterly Review* 49 (1958–59): 251.
11. Zeitlin, "Proselytes and Proselytism," p. 877.
12. Ibid., p. 878.
13. Ibid., p. 874; cf. Zeitlin, "Who Is a Jew?" pp. 248 f.
14. Moore, *Judaism*, vol. 1, p. 337.
15. Solomon Zeitlin, "The Jews: Race, Nation or Religion—Which?" *Jewish Quarterly Review* 26 (1935–36): 331.
16. Ibid., pp. 327–33; cf. Zeitlin, "Proselytes and Proselytism," pp. 872 f.; Deut. 23:4; Neh. 13:13.
17. H. L. Poppers, "Déclassé in the Babylonian Jewish Community," *Jewish Social Studies* 20 (1958): 154; cf. *Horayot* 3:8.

CHAPTER 9

1. A. D. Nock, *Conversion* (London, 1961), pp. 6 f.
2. Ibid., p. 13.
3. Ibid., p. 185.
4. Cf. Horace 1. f. 140–43; Seneca, *De Civdei* 6.11; George La Pina, "Foreign Groups in Rome During the First Centuries of the Empire," *Harvard Theological Review* 20 (1927).

5. Emil Schürer, *A History of the Jewish People in the Time of Jesus Christ,* (Edinburgh, 1905), vol. 3, pp. 270 f.

6. Robert Wilde, *The Treatment of the Jews in the Greek Christian Writers of the First Three Centuries* (Washington, 1949), pp. 20 ff., 74 ff.

7. H. Graetz, *History of the Jews* (Philadelphia, 1893), vol. 2, p. 306.

8. Ibid., p. 136.

9. Ibid., p. 137.

10. Norman Bentwich, "The Rightfulness of the Jews in the Roman Empire," *Jewish Quarterly Review,* o.s. 6 (1915–16).

11. James Parkes, "Christian Influence on the Status of the Jews in Europe," *Historia Judaica* 1 (1938): 31.

12. N. Idris Bell, *Cults and Creeds in Graeco-Roman Egypt* (Liverpool, 1953), p. 37.

13. Simon Davis, *Race Relations in Ancient Egypt* (London, 1951), p. 113 ff.

14. James Parkes, *The Conflict of the Church and the Synagogue* (Cleveland, 1961), p. 24.

15. A. N. Sherwin-White, *Racial Prejudice in Imperial Rome* (Cambridge, 1967), p. 87.

16. Ibid., p. 92; cf. pp. 86–101.

17. Davis, *Race Relations in Ancient Egypt,* p. 117.

18. Ibid., p. 118.

19. Ibid., p. 158.

20. G. La Pina, "Foreign Groups in Rome," p. 387.

21. Ibid., p. 392.

22. Wilde, *Jews in the Greek Christian Writers,* p. 25.

CHAPTER 10

1. Simeon L. Guterman, *Religious Toleration and Persecution in Ancient Rome* (London, 1951), p. 114.

2. Ibid., p. 75.

3. Nock, *Conversion,* p. 210.

4. Ibid., p. 211.

5. Ibid., p. 233.

6. Ibid., p. 236.

7. Ibid., p. 253.

8. La Pina, "Foreign Groups in Rome," p. 384.

9. Ibid., p. 393.

10. James Parkes, *The Foundations of Judaism and Christianity* (Chicago, 1960), p. 319, n. 16.

11. Parkes, "Christian Influence on the Status of the Jews," p. 32.

12. Bamberger, *Proselytism in the Talmudic Period,* p. 3.

CHAPTER 11

1. W. Montgomery Watt, *Islam and the Integration of Society* (London, 1961), pp. 9 and 15.

2. S. D. Goitein, *Jews and Arabs* (New York, 1955), p. 64.

CHAPTER 12

1. Baron, *Social and Religious History,* vol. 4, p. 9.
2. Louis Israel Newman, *Jewish Influence on Christian Reform Movements* (New York, 1925), pp. 1 f.
3. Yitzhak Baer, *A History of the Jews in Christian Spain* (Philadelphia, 1961), vol. 1, p. 21.
4. Solomon Grayzel, *The Church and the Jews in the XIIIth Century,* rev. ed. (New York, 1966), p. 199.
5. Baer, *Jews in Christian Spain,* vol. 2, p. 10.
6. I. Levy, *Les Juifs et l'Inquisition* (Paris, 1881), p. 7.

CHAPTER 13

1. Jacob Katz, *Exclusiveness and Tolerance* (London, 1961), pp. 11 f., 67 f.
2. Ibid., pp. 143–46.
3. Albert M. Hyamson, *The Sephardim of England* (London, 1951), pp. 19, 22.
4. Ibid., pp. 29, 65 ff., 174 ff., 329, 358.
5. Henry E. A. I. Phillips, "An Early Stuart Judaizing Sect," *Transactions of the Jewish Historical Society of England* 15 (1946): 63–72.
6. Ben Zion Wacholder, "Cases of Proselytizing in the Tosafist Responsa," *Jewish Quarterly Review* 51 (1960–61): 290.
7. Ibid., pp. 290 ff.
8. Ibid., pp. 297 ff.
9. *Sefer Hasidim* (Berlin, 1924), no. 214, p. 77.
10. Irving A. Agus, *Rabbi Meir of Rothenburg* (Philadelphia, 1947), vol. 2, p. 545; cf. pp. 666 f.
11. Ben Zion Wacholder, "Attitudes Towards Proselytizing in the Classical Halakah," *Historia Judaica* 20 (1958): 87.

CHAPTER 14

1. Wacholder, "Proselytizing in the Tosafist Responsa," p. 314.
2. Ben Zion Wacholder, "The Halakah and the Proselytizing of Slaves During the Gaonic Era," *Historia Judaica* 18 (1956): 106.
3. Wacholder, "Proselytizing in the Tosafist Responsa," p. 313.
4. Salo W. Baron, *History and Jewish Historians* (Philadelphia, 1964), p. 50.
5. Samuel Oppenheim, "The Early History of the Jews in New York, 1654–1664," *Publications of the American Jewish Historical Society* 18 (1909): 17.
6. Wacholder, "Proselytizing of Slaves," p. 313.
7. Jacob Mann, "The Responsa of the Babylonian Geonim as a Source of Jewish History," *Jewish Quarterly Review,* o.s. 10 (1919): 148.
8. Wacholder, "Proselytizing of Slaves," p. 101.
9. S. D. Goitein, *A Mediterranean Society* (Berkeley and Los Angeles, 1967), p. 136.
10. Ibid., p. 137.

11. Lancelot Addison, *The Present State of the Jews* (London, 1675), p. 67.

12. Allen Cabaniss, "Bodo-Eleazar: A Famous Jewish Convert," *Jewish Quarterly Review* 43 (1952–53): 313–28; Baron, *Social and Religious History*, vol. 4, p. 9; Baer, *Jews in Christian Spain*, vol. 1, p. 24.

13. Baron, *Social and Religious History*, vol. 4, p. 66.

14. Ibid., vol. 5, p. 113.

15. Cecil Roth, *A History of the Jews of England* (Oxford, 1964), pp. 41, 83.

16. Norman Golb, "Notes on the Conversion of European Christians in the 11th Century," *Journal of Jewish Studies* 16 (1965): 69 ff.

17. Wacholder, "Proselytizing in the Tosafist Responsa," p. 304.

18. Cecil Roth, "New Notes on Pre-Emancipation Jewish Artists," *Hebrew Union College Annual* 17 (1942–43): 501.

19. Baron, *Social and Religious History*, vol. 2, p. 57.

20. Ibid., vol. 5, p. 114.

21. Cecil Roth, "Immanuel Aboab's Proselytization of the Marranos," *Jewish Quarterly Review* 23 (1932–33): 137.

22. Baron, *Social and Religious History*, vol. 2, p. 57.

23. Baer, *Jews in Christian Spain*, vol. 2, p. 10.

24. Jacob Mann, *Texts and Studies* (Cincinnati, 1931), vol. 1, p. 31.

25. Baron, *Social and Religious History*, vol. 2, p. 57.

26. S. Singer, "Early Translations and Translators of the Jewish Liturgy in England," *Transactions of the Jewish Historical Society in England* 3 (1899): 39 ff.

27. Hans-Joachim Schoeps, "Philosemitism in the Baroque Period," *Jewish Quarterly Review* 47 (1956–57): 142.

28. Cecil Roth, "Leone da Modena and England," *Transactions of the Jewish Historical Society of England* 11 (1928): 215.

29. Salo W. Baron, *The Russian Jew Under Tsars and Soviets* (New York, 1964), p. 13.

CHAPTER 15

1. Howard Becker, *Through Values to Social Interpretation* (Durham, N.C., 1950), p. 112.

2. Miriam Beard, "Anti-Semitism, Product of Economic Myths," in *Jews in a Gentile World*, ed. Isacque Graeber and Steuart H. Britt (New York, 1942), pp. 387 ff.

3. Max Weber, *General Economic History* (Glencoe, Ill., 1950), pp. 319 f.

4. Guido Kisch, *The Jews of Medieval Germany* (Chicago, 1949), pp. 319 f.

5. Ibid., p. 323; Miriam Beard, *A History of the Business Man* (New York, 1938), p. 318.

6. Kisch, *Jews of Medieval Germany*, p. 318.

7. Irving A. Agus, *Urban Civilization in Pre-Crusade Europe* (Leiden, 1965), vol. 1, pp. 7 f.

8. Kisch, *Jews of Medieval Germany*, p. 320.

9. Ibid., pp. 320 f.; cf. Guido Kisch, "The Jew's Function in the Medieval Evolution of Economic Life," *Historia Judaica* 6 (1944): p. 7.

10. Kisch, "Jew's Function," pp. 8–12.

11. Beard, History of the Business Man, pp. 119 ff.; "Anti-Semitism," pp. 372–88.

12. Benjamin N. Nelson, *The Idea of Usury: From Tribal Brotherhood to Universal Otherhood* (Princeton, N.J., 1949), p. xxi.

13. Ibid., p. 12.

14. Ibid., p. 54.

15. Ibid., p. 76.

16. Morris S. Goodblatt, *Jewish Life in Turkey in the XVIth Century* (New York, 1952), p. 212.

CHAPTER 17

1. Schürer, *Jewish People in the Time of Jesus Christ*, vol. 2, pp. 326-32.

2. Zeitlin, "The Jews: Race, Nation or Religion," p. 327.

3. Ibid., p. 329.

4. Ibid., p. 331.

CHAPTER 18

1. Jacob Neusner, "The Jews in Pagan Armenia," *Journal of the American Oriental Society* 84 (1964): 240.

2. George Rawlinson, *The Sixth Oriental Monarchy* (London, 1873), pp. 240–47; Neilson C. Debevoise, *A Political History of Parthia* (Chicago, 1938), pp. xxxix f., 111–20, 145, 161 ff., 177 f., 185 f., 230, 236, 242, 255 f.

3. Citations above from Josephus, Rawlinson, and Debevoise. Also Neusner, "Jews in Pagan Armenia," pp. 234–40; "Conversion of Adiabene to Judaism," *Journal of Biblical Literature* 83 (1964): 60–65; *A History of the Jews in Babylonia* (Leiden, 1965), vol. 1, pp. 51–66; Paul E. Kahle, *The Cairo Geniza* (London, 1947), pp. 186 ff.

CHAPTER 19

1. Philip K. Hitti, *History of the Arabs* (London, 1960), p. 61.

2. Baron, *Social and Religious History*, vol. 3, pp. 65, 70.

3. Joseph Horovitz, "Judaeo-Arabic Relations in Pre-Islamic Times," *Islamic Culture* 3 (1928): 177 f., 186–91.

4. David S. Margoliouth, *The Relations between Arabs and Israelites Prior to the Rise of Islam* (London, 1924), p. 71.

5. Ibid., p. 63.

6. Axel Moberg, *The Book of the Himyarites* (Lund, 1924), pp. xi et passim.

7. Baron, *Social and Religious History*, vol. 3, pp. 65–69.

8. H. Z. Hirschberg, *Israel in Arabia* (in Hebrew) (Tel Aviv, 1946), pp. 69 f., 101.

9. Margoliouth, *Jews and Arabs Prior to the Rise of Islam*, p. 64.

CHAPTER 20

1. H. Z. Hirschberg, "The Problem of the Judaized Berbers," *Journal of African History* 4 (1963): 317.

2. Ibid., p. 329.
3. Ibid.
4. Ibid., p. 335.
5. Ibid., p. 338.
6. L. Cabot Briggs, *The Living Races of the Sahara Desert* (Cambridge, Mass., 1958), p. 174.
7. Stephan Gsell, *Histoire Ancienne de l'Afrique du Nord* (Paris, 1921), vol. 1, p. 281; N. Kossovitch, *Anthropologie et Groupes Sanguins des Populations du Maroc* (Paris, 1953), pp. 457 f.
8. Carleton Coon, *Races of Europe* (New York, 1939), p. 443; M. J. Herskovits, in *The Jews*, ed. L. Finkelstein, p. 1153; Andre Chouraqui, *Les Juifs d'Afrique du Nord* (Paris, 1952), pp. 26, 38 ff.; Milton Jacobs, *A Study in Culture Stability and Change: The Moroccan Jewess* (Washington, 1965).

CHAPTER 21

1. D. M. Dunlop, *The History of the Jewish Khazars* (Princeton, 1954), p. 144.
2. Zvi Ankori, *Karaites in Byzantium* (New York, 1959), p. 70.
3. Solomon Schechter, "An Unknown Khazar Document," *Jewish Quarterly Review*, o.s. 3 (1912–13): 183.
4. Dunlop, *History of the Jewish Khazars*, p. 125.
5. Ibid., p. 170.
6. Ibid.
7. J. B. Bury, *A History of the Eastern Roman Empire* (London, 1912), p. 406.
8. Louis Greenberg, *The Jews in Russia* (New Haven, 1965), p. 1.
9. Rudolf Lowenthal, "The Judeo-Tats in the Caucasus," *Historia Judaica* 16 (1952): 61 ff.
10. M. Postan, ed., *The Cambridge Economic History* (Cambridge, 1952), vol. 2, pp. 91 f., 488.
11. Dunlop, *History of the Jewish Khazars*, pp. 194 f.
12. J. M. Hussey, ed., *The Cambridge Medieval History* (Cambridge, 1966), vol. 4, p. 111.
13. Ibid., p. 485.
14. Ibid., p. 487.
15. Salo W. Baron, *Russian Jew Under Tsars and Soviets*, p. 4.
16. Louis I. Rabinowitz, *Jewish Merchant Adventurers* (London, 1948), pp. 78 f.; Rudolf Lowenthal, Review of *Jewish Merchant Adventurers*, by L. Rabinowitz, *Historia Judaica* 11 (1949): 163 ff.; Zvi Ankori, Review of *The History of the Jewish Khazars*, by J. M. Dunlop, *Judaism* 5 (1956): 188.
17. *Encyclopaedia Britannica*, 13th ed., vol. 15, p. 774.
18. Dunlop, *History of the Jewish Khazars*, p. 230.
19. Ibid., p. 241.
20. Ibid., p. 250.
21. Ibid., pp. 222 ff.
22. Baron, *Social and Religious History*, vol. 3, p. 200.
23. *Cambridge Economic History*, vol. 2, p. 287.
24. Dunlop, *History of the Jewish Khazars*, p. 221.
25. Baron, *Social and Religious History*, vol. 3, p. 200.

26. Ibid., p. 206.
27. Ibid., p. 215.
28. Jan Czekanowski, "Anthropological Structure of the Jewish People in the Light of Polish Analyses," *Jewish Journal of Sociology* 2 (1963): 263 ff.
29. Adam Vetulani, "The Jews of Medieval Poland," *Jewish Journal of Sociology* 4 (1962): 274.
30. Ankori, *Karaites in Byzantium*, p. 74.
31. J. Brutzkus, "The Khazar Origin of Ancient Kiev," *Slavonic and East European Review* 22 (1944): 111, 124.

CHAPTER 22

1. Edward Ullendorff, *The Ethiopians: An Introduction to Country and People*, 2nd ed. (London, 1965), pp. 97–100, 111 f.
2. Henry A. Stern, *Wanderings Among the Falashas in Abyssinia* (London, 1862); J. M. Flad, *The Falashas of Abyssinia* (London, 1869); *Jewish Encyclopedia*, vol. 5, pp. 327 f.; Wolf Leslau, *The Falasha Anthology* (New Haven, 1951).
3. *Jerusalem Post Weekly*, December 26, 1972, p. 4.

CHAPTER 23

1. This estimate was made in a personal communication by Bernard Lazerwitz, Research Professor, University of Missouri (Columbia).
2. Erich Rosenthal, "Studies of Jewish Intermarriage in the United States," *American Jewish Yearbook,* vol. 64 (New York, 1963), p. 8.
3. Ibid., p. 9. Erich Rosenthal, "Acculturation Without Assimilation—The Jewish Community of Chicago, Illinois," *American Journal of Sociology* 66 (1960–61) 275, 281.
4. Ibid., pp. 275, 286.
5. Unless otherwise noted, statistics of rates of intermarriage are included in table 1. Notes 6–21 below refer to sources of data in the table.
6. Uriah Z. Engelman, "Intermarriage Among Jews in Germany, U.S.S.R., and Switzerland," *Jewish Social Studies* 11 (1940): 157.
7. Jacob Barr and Werner J. Cahnman, "Interfaith Marriages in Switzerland," in *Intermarriage and Jewish Life: A Symposium,* ed. Werner J. Cahnman (New York, 1960), p. 53.
8. Moshe Davis, "Mixed Marriage in Western Jewry: Historical Background to the Jewish Response," *CCAR Journal* 10 (1962): 17.
9. Louis Rosenberg, "Intermarriage in Canada," in Cahnman, *Intermarriage and Jewish Life,* p. 62.
10. Paul Glick, "Intermarriage and Fertility Patterns Among Persons in Major Religious Groups," *Eugenics Quarterly* 7 (1960): 34.
11. Andrew Greeley. Follow-up of *The Great Aspirations Study* (Report No. 82, National Opinion Research Center, University of Chicago), by James A. Davis and Norman Bradburn (Chicago, 1961). Personal communication.
12. Theodore Lenn and associates, *Rabbi and Synagogue in Reform Judaism* (West Hartford, Conn., 1972), p. 217.

13. Marshall Sklare, *America's Jews* (New York, 1971), p. 184.
14. Ruby Jo Reeves Kennedy, "Single or Triple Melting Pot? Intermarriage Trends in New Haven, 1870–1940," *American Journal of Sociology* 44 (1944): 333.
15. Herschel Shanks, "Jewish-Gentile Intermarriage: Facts and Trends," *Commentary* 26 (1953): 370.
16. Ruby Jo Reeves Kennedy, "What Has Social Science to Say About Intermarriage?" in Cahnman, *Intermarriage and Jewish Life,* p. 29.
17. Erich Rosenthal, "Some Recent Studies About the Extent of Jewish Outmarriage in the U.S.A.," in Cahnman, *Intermarriage and Jewish Life,* p. 86.
18. Sidney Goldstein and Calvin Goldscheider, "Social and Demographic Aspects of Jewish Intermarriage," *Social Problems* 13 (1966): 389.
19. Bernard Lazerwitz, "Intermarriage and Conversion," *Jewish Journal of Sociology* 13 (1971): 34 f.
20. Erich Rosenthal, "Jewish Intermarriage in Indiana," *American Jewish Yearbook,* vol. 68 (New York, 1967), p. 263.
21. Fred Massarik and Alvin Chenkin, "United States National Jewish Population Study: A First Report," *American Jewish Yearbook,* vol. 74 (1973), p. 295.
22. Ibid., p. 266.
23. Rosenthal, "Acculturation without Assimilation," p. 288.
24. Rosenthal, "Jewish Intermarriage in the United States," p. 51.
25. Rosenthal, "Jewish Intermarriage in Indiana."
26. Morris Fishberg, *The Jews* (New York, 1911), p. 214.
27. Rosenthal, "Jewish Intermarriage in the United States," p. 31.
28. Goldstein and Goldscheider, "Social and Demographic Aspects of Jewish Intermarriage," p. 398.
29. Sklare, *America's Jews,* p. 189.
30. Glick, "Intermarriage and Fertility Patterns," p. 32, 34, 37.
31. Goldstein and Goldscheider, "Social and Demographic Aspects of Jewish Intermarriage," pp. 397 f.
32. Davis, "Mixed Marriage in Western Jewry," p. 6.
33. Ibid., pp. 6 f.
34. Ibid., p. 7.
35. Glick, "Intermarriage and Fertility Patterns," p. 35; Kennedy, "What Has Social Science to Say About Intermarriage?" p. 31; Rosenberg, "Intermarriage in Canada," p. 62.
36. Marshall Sklare and Joseph Greenblum, *Jewish Identity on the Suburban Frontier* (New York, 1967), pp. 309, 311, 314, 315.
37. Lazerwitz, "Intermarriage and Conversion," p. 60.
38. Maria H. Levinson and Daniel J. Levinson, "Jews Who Intermarry: Socio-Psychological Bases of Ethnic Identity and Change," *YIVO Annual of Jewish Social Science* 12 (1958–59): 130.
39. Sklare, *America's Jews,* p. 183.
40. Ibid., p. 203.
41. Abraham Shusterman, "The Last Two Centuries," in *Conversion to Judaism: A History and Analysis,* ed. David Max Eichhorn (New York, 1965), p. 137.
42. Davis, "Mixed Marriage in Western Jewry," p. 16.
43. *Encyclopedia Judaica,* vol. 3, col. 421.

44. Shusterman, "The Last Two Centuries," p. 170 f.
45. Ibid., p. 141.
46. Ibid., p. 143.
47. Ibid., p. 148.
48. Ibid., pp. 148, 165 ff.
49. Lenn, *Rabbi and Synagogue*, pp. 184 f.
50. Simon N. Herman, *Israelis and Jews* (New York, 1970), p. 255.
51. Sklare and Greenblum, *Jewish Identity on the Suburban Frontier*, pp. 272 f.
52. John Oswald Simon, "Missionary Judaism," *Jewish Quarterly Review*, o.s. 5 (1893): 665, 669, 673.
53. John Oswald Simon, "The Mission of Israel," *Fortnightly Review*, n.s. 60 (London, 1896): 578 f., 582 f., 586.
54. John Oswald Simon, "The Mission of Israel," *Jewish Quarterly Review*, o.s. 9 (1897): 177–223; "The Mission of Judaism: A Reply," *Jewish Quarterly Review*, o.s. 9 (1897): 403–28.
55. Shusterman, "The Last Two Centuries," p. 164; *Encyclopedia Judaica*, vol. 13, col. 1191.
56. Shusterman, "The Last Two Centuries," p. 171; *Encyclopedia Judaica*, vol. 13, col. 1192.
57. Robert Gordis, "Has the Time Arrived for Jewish Missionaries?" *National Jewish Monthly*, March 1958, pp. 6 f., 24 ff.
58. *The Jewish Information Society: Its Background, Purpose and Program* (Chicago, 1959); Shusterman, "The Last Two Centuries," p. 169; *Jewish Information* (Chicago, 1960–69).
59. Leo Baeck, "The Mission of Judaism," *World Union for Progressive Judaism, Report Sixth International Conference* (London, 1949), p. 74.
60. Allen S. Maller, "The Mission of Israel and Reform Theology," *Reconstructionist* 32 (1966): 16.
61. Ibid., pp. 19, 21.
62. Allen S. Maller, "Mixed Marriage and Reform Rabbis," *Judaism* 24 (Winter 1975): 39.
63. David Max Eichhorn, "Conversion to Judaism by Reform and Conservative Rabbis," *Jewish Social Studies* 16 (1954): 301.
64. Ibid., p. 302.
65. Albert I. Gordon, *The Nature of Conversion* (Boston, 1967), p. 5.
66. Allen S. Maller, "From Gentile into Jew," *Reconstructionist* 33 (June 23, 1967): 25, 27.
67. Goldstein and Goldscheider, "Social and Demographic Aspects of Jewish Intermarriage," p. 393.
68. Lenn, *Rabbi and Synagogue*, pp. 217 f.
69. Massarik and Chenkin, "United States National Jewish Population Study," p. 292.
70. *Encyclopedia Judaica*, vol. 13, cols. 1191 f.
71. Gordon, *Nature of Conversion*, p. 5.
72. Richard Rubenstein, "Intermarriage and Conversion," *Reconstructionist* 28 (April 29, 1962): 20.
73. Lazarwitz, "Intermarriage and Conversion," pp. 42, 48, 52, 58 f.

74. Erich Rosenthal, "Some Recent Studies About the Extent of Jewish Out-marriage in the U.S.A.," in Cahnman, *Intermarriage and Jewish Life.*

75. David Max Eichhorn, "Conversion: Requirements and Results," in Cahnman, *Intermarriage and Jewish Life*, p. 120.

76. Lazerwitz, "Intermarriage and Conversion," p. 58.

77. Lenn, *Rabbi and Synagogue*, p. 261.

78. *Encyclopedia Judaica*, vol. 14, cols. 843 f.

79. Mordecai Roshwald, "Marginal Gentiles in Israel," *Judaism* 24 (Winter 1975): 7–11.

80. *Encyclopedia Judaica*, vol. 4, cols. 1068 ff.; Howard Brotz, *The Black Jews of Harlem* (New York); Murray Polnar, "Being Black and Jewish," *National Jewish Monthly* (October, 1972): 38–43.

81. Robert G. Weisbrod, "Israel and the Black Hebrew Israelites," *Judaism* 24 (Winter 1975): 23–38.

82. *Encyclopedia Judaica*, vol. 10, col. 398.

83. Ibid., cols. 397, 399 ff.

84. Frank Peters, "Jews of Mexico," *St. Louis Post-Dispatch Pictures*, May 14, 1967, pp. 10–15.

Bibliography

Addison, Lancelot. *The Present State of the Jews.* London, 1675.

Agus, Irving A. *Rabbi Meir of Rothenburg.* Philadelphia, 1947.

———. *Urban Civilization in Pre-Crusade Europe.* Leiden, 1965.

Anderson, G. W. "Some Aspects of the Uppsala School of Old Testament Study." *Harvard Theological Review* 43 (1950): 239–56.

Ankori, Zvi, *Karaites in Byzantium.* New York, 1959.

———. Review of *The History of the Jewish Khazars,* by D. M. Dunlop. *Judaism* 5 (1956): 185–88.

Babylonian Talmud. Edited by I. Epstein and A. Cohen. 19 vols. London 1938–65.

Baeck, Leo. "The Mission of Judaism." In *World Union for Progressive Judaism, Report Sixth International Conference.* London, 1949.

Baer, Yitzhak. *A History of the Jews in Christian Spain.* Philadelphia, 1961.

Bamberger, Bernard. *Proselytism in the Talmud Period.* Rev. ed. New York, 1968.

Baron, Salo W. *History and Jewish Historians.* Philadelphia, 1964.

———. *The Russian Jew Under Tsars and Soviets.* New York, 1964.

———. *A Social and Religious History of the Jews.* New York, 1937–57.

Beard, Miriam. *A History of the Business Man.* New York, 1938.

Becker, Howard, *Through Values to Social Interpretation.* Durham, N.C., 1950.

Bell, H. Idris. *Cults and Creeds in the Graeco-Roman Egypt.* Liverpool, 1953.

Bentwich, Norman. "The Rightfulness of the Jews in the Roman Empire." *Jewish Quarterly Review* 6 (1915): 325–36.

Berman, Julius. *Jews and Intermarriage: A Study in Personality and Culture.* New York, 1968.

Braude, William G. *Jewish Proselyting.* Providence, R.I., 1940.

Briggs, L. Cabot. *The Living Races of the Sahara Desert.* Cambridge, Mass., 1958.

Bright, John. *Early Israel in Recent History Writing.* London, 1956.

161

————. *A History of Israel.* Philadelphia, 1959.

Brotz, Howard. *Black Jews of Harlem.* New York, 1964.

Brutzkus, J. "The Khazar Origin of Ancient Kiev." *Slavonic and East European Review* 22 (1944): 108–24.

Bury, J. B. *A History of the Eastern Roman Empire.* London, 1912.

Cabaniss, Allan. "Bodo-Eleazar: A Famous Jewish Convert." *Jewish Quarterly Review* 43 (1952–53): 313–28.

Cahnman, Werner J., ed. *Intermarriage and Jewish Life: A Symposium.* New York, 1960.

Chouraqui, André. *Les Juifs d'Afrique du Nord.* Paris, 1952.

Coon, Carleton, *Races of Europe.* New York, 1939.

Czekanowski, Jan. "Anthropological Structure of the Jewish People in the Light of Polish Analyses." *Jewish Journal of Sociology* 2 (1960).

Davis, Moshe. "Mixed Marriage in Western Jewry: Historical Background to the Jewish Response." *CCAR Journal* 10 (1962): 2–47.

Davis, Simon. *Race Relations in Ancient Egypt.* London, 1951.

Debevoise, Neilson C. *A Political History of Parthia.* Chicago, 1938.

de Vaux, Roland. *Ancient Israel.* New York, 1965.

Dunlop, D. M. *The History of the Jewish Khazars.* Princeton, N.J., 1954.

Eichhorn, David Max, ed. *Conversion to Judaism: A History and Analysis.* New York, 1965.

————. "Conversions to Judaism by Reform and Conservative Rabbis." *Jewish Social Studies* 16 (1954): 299–318.

Engelman, Uriah Z. "Intermarriage Among Jews in Germany, USSR and Switzerland." *Jewish Social Studies* 2 (1940): 157–78.

Engnell, I. *Gamla Testamentet. En traditionshistorisk inledning,* I. Uppsala and Stockholm, 1945. Cited in G. W. Anderson, "Some Aspects of the Uppsala School of Old Testament Study," *Harvard Theological Review* 43 (1950): 239–56.

Epstein, Louis M. *Marriage Laws in the Bible and the Talmud.* Cambridge, Mass., 1942.

Finkelstein, Louis, ed. *The Jews: Their History, Culture and Religion.* New York, 1949.

————. *The Pharisees: The Sociological Background of Their Faith.* Philadelphia, 1946.

Fishberg, Morris. *The Jews.* New York, 1911.

Flad, J. M. *The Falashas of Abyssinia.* London, 1869.

Glick, Paul. "Intermarriage and Fertility Patterns Among Persons in Major Religious Groups." *Eugenics Quarterly* 7 (1960): 31–38.

Goitein, S. D. *Jews and Arabs.* New York, 1955.

————. *A Mediterranean Society.* Berkeley and Los Angeles, 1967.

Golb, Norman. "Notes on the Conversion of European Christians in the 11th Century." *Journal of Jewish Studies* 16 (1965): 69–74.

Goldstein, Sidney, and Goldscheider, Calvin. "Social and Demographic Aspects of Jewish Intermarriages." *Social Problems* 13 (1966): 386–99.

Goodblatt, Morris S. *Jewish Life in Turkey in the XVI Century.* New York, 1952.

Gordis, Robert. "Has the Time Arrived for Jewish Missionaries?" *National Jewish Monthly,* March 1958, pp. 6–7, 24–27.

Gordon, Albert I. *The Nature of Conversion.* Boston, 1967.

Gottwald, Norman. *A Light to the Nations.* New York, 1959.

Graeber, Isacque, and Britt, Steuart H., eds. *Jews in a Gentile World.* New York, 1942.

Graetz, H. *History of the Jews.* Philadelphia, 1893.

Grayzel, Solomon. *The Church and the Jews in the XIIIth Century.* Rev. ed. New York, 1966.

Greeley, Andrew. Follow-up study of *The Great Aspirations Study.* Personal communication on a follow-up study of *The Great Aspirations Study* (Report No. 82, National Opinion Research Center, University of Chicago) by James A. Davis and Norman Bradborn (Chicago, 1961).

Greenberg, Louis. *The Jews in Russia.* New Haven, 1965.

Gsell, Stephan. *Histoiré Ancienne de L'Afrique du Nord.* Paris, 1921.

Guterman, Simeon L. *Religious Toleration and Persecution in Ancient Rome.* London, 1951.

Heer, David. "The Trend of Interfaith Marriages in Canada." *American Sociological Review* 27 (1962): 245–50.

Herman, Simon N. *Israelis and Jews.* New York, 1970.

Hirschberg, H. Z. *Israel in Arabia.* (in Hebrew) Tel Aviv, 1946.

———. "The Problem of the Judaized Berbers." *Journal of African History* 4 (1963): 313–39.

Hitti, Philip K. *History of the Arabs.* London, 1960.

Horovitz, Joseph. "Judaeo-Arabic Relations in Pre-Islamic Times," *Islamic Culture* 3 (1929): 161–99.

Hussey, J. M., ed. *The Cambridge Medieval History,* 4. Cambridge, 1966.

Hyamson, Albert M. *The Sephardim of England.* London, 1951.

Jacobs, Milton. *A Study in Culture Stability and Change: The Moroccan Jewess.* Washington, 1965.

Jewish Information Society: Its Background, Purpose and Program. Chicago, 1959.

Josephus, Flavius. *Works.* Translated by H. St. J. Thackeray, Ralph Marcus, Allen Wikgren, and L. H. Feldman. 9 vols. Cambridge, Mass., 1926-65.

Kahle, Paul E. *The Cairo Geniza.* London, 1947.

Katz, Jacob. *Exclusiveness and Tolerance.* London, 1961.

Kaufmann, Yehezkel. *The Biblical Account of the Conquest of Palestine.* Jerusalem, 1953.

———. *The Religion of Israel.* Chicago, 1960.

Kautsky, Karl. *Are the Jews a Race?* London, 1926.

———. *Foundations of Christianity.* London, 1925.

Kennedy, Ruby Jo Reeves. "Single or Triple Melting Pot? Intermarriage

Trends in New Haven, 1870–1940." *American Journal of Sociology* 44 (1944): 331–39.

Kisch, Guido. "The Jew's Function in the Medieval Evolution of Economic Life." *Historia Judaica* 6 (1944): 1–12.

———. *The Jews of Medieval Germany*. Chicago, 1949.

Klausner, Joseph. *From Jesus to Paul*. London, 1946.

———. *The Messianic Idea in Israel*. New York, 1955.

Kossovitch, N. *Anthropologie et Groupes Sanguins des Populations du Maroc.* Paris, 1953.

LaPina, George. "Foreign Groups in Rome During the First Centuries of the Empire." *Harvard Theological Review* 20 (1927): 183–483.

Lazerwitz, Bernard. "Intermarriage and Conversion." *Jewish Journal of Sociology* 13 (1971): 41–63.

Lenn, Theodore, and associates. *Rabbi and Synagogue in Reform Judaism*. West Hartford, Conn., 1972.

Leslau, Wolf. *The Falasha Anthology*. New Haven, 1951.

Levinson, Marcia, and Levinson, Daniel. "Jews Who Intermarry: Socio-Psychological Bases of Ethnic Identity and Change." *YIVO Annual of Jewish Social Science* 12 (1958): 106–28.

Levy, I. *Les Juifs et l'Inquisition*. Paris, 1881.

Lowenthal, Rudolf. "The Judeo-Tats in the Caucasus." *Historia Judaica* 14 (1952): 61–82.

———. Review of *Jewish Merchant Adventurers*, by Louis I. Rabinowitz. *Historia Judaica* 11 (1949): 163–65.

McCown, C. C. "The Density of Population in Ancient Palestine." *Journal of Biblical Literature* 46 (1947): 425–36.

Maller, Allen S. "From Gentile into Jew." *Reconstructionist* 33 (1967): 24–27.

———. "The Mission of Israel and Reform Theology." *Reconstructionist* 32 (1966): 16–21.

———. "Mixed Marriage and Reform Rabbis." *Judaism* 24 (Winter 1975): 39–48.

Mann, Jacob. "The Responsa of the Babylonian Geonim as a Source of Jewish History." *Jewish Quarterly Review*, o.s. 10 (1919): 121–52.

———. *Texts and Studies*. Cincinnati, 1931.

Marcus, Ralph. "The *Sebomenoi* in Josephus." *Jewish Social Studies* 14 (1953): 247–50.

Margoliouth, David S. *The Relations Between Arabs and Israelites Prior to the Rise of Islam*. London, 1924.

Massarik, Fred, and Chenkin, Alvin. "United States National Jewish Population Study: A First Report." In *American Jewish Yearbook*, vol. 74, pp. 264–315. New York, 1973.

Meek, T. J. "The Translation of *Ger* in the Hexateuch and Its Bearing on the Documentary Theory." *Journal of Biblical Literature* 49 (1930): 172–80.

Mishnah. Translated by Herbert Danby. London, 1938.

Moberg, Axel. *The Book of the Himyarites.* Lund, 1924.

Montefiore, C. G., and Loewe, H. *A Rabbinic Anthology.* London, 1938.

Moore, George Foot. *Judaism.* Cambridge, Mass., 1932.

Nelson, Benjamin N. *The Idea of Usury: From Tribal Brotherhood to Universal Otherhood.* Princeton, N.J., 1949.

Neusner, Jacob. "Conversion of Adiabene to Judaism." *Journal of Biblical Literature* 83 (1964): 60–66.

————. *A History of the Jews in Babylonia.* Leiden, 1965.

————. "The Jews in Pagan Armenia." *Journal of the American Oriental Society* 84 (1964): 230–40.

Newman, Louis Israel. *Jewish Influence on Christian Reform Movements.* New York, 1925.

Nock, A. D. *Conversion.* London, 1961.

Noth, Martin. *The History of Israel.* London, 1958.

Oppenheim, Samuel. "The Early History of the Jews in New York, 1654–1664." *Publications of the American Jewish Historical Society* 18 (1909): 1–92.

Orlinsky, Harry M., and Snaith, Norman H. *Studies on the Second Part of the Book of Isaiah.* Leiden, 1967.

Parkes, James. "Christian Influence on the Status of the Jews in Europe." *Historia Judaica* 1 (1938): 31–38.

————. *The Conflict of the Church and the Synagogue.* Cleveland, 1961.

————. *The Foundations of Judaism and Christianity.* Chicago, 1960.

Pedersen, Johannes. *Israel: Its Life and Culture.* London, 1926.

Phillips, Henry E. A. I. "An Early Stuart Judaizing Sect." *Transactions of the Jewish Historical Society of England* 15 (1946): 63–72.

Philo Judaeus. *Works.* Translated by Ralph Marcus, F. H. Colson, G. H. Whitaker, and J. W. Earp. 12 vols. Cambridge, Mass., 1929–62.

Polner, Murray, "Being Black and Jewish." *National Jewish Monthly* 87 (October 1972): 38–43.

Peters, Frank. "Jews of Mexico." *St. Louis Post-Dispatch Pictures,* May 14, 1967, pp. 10–15.

Poppers, H. L. "Declassé in the Babylonian Jewish Community." *Jewish Social Studies* 20 (1958): 153–79.

Postan, M., ed. *The Cambridge Economic History,* vol. 2. Cambridge, 1952.

Rabinowitz, Louis I. *Jewish Merchant Adventurers.* London, 1948.

Ramsey, Paul, ed. *Religion.* Englewood Cliffs, N.J., 1965.

Rawlinson, George. *The Sixth Oriental Monarchy.* London, 1873.

Rosenthal, Erich. "Acculturation Without Assimilation—The Jewish Community of Chicago, Illinois." *American Journal of Sociology* 66 (1960–61): 275–88.

————. "Jewish Intermarriage in Indiana." In *American Jewish Yearbook,* vol. 68, pp. 243–64. New York, 1967.

————. "Studies of Jewish Intermarriage in the United States." In *American Jewish Yearbook*, vol. 64, pp. 3–53. New York, 1963.

Roshwald, Mordecai. "Marginal Gentiles in Israel." *Judaism* 24 (Winter 1975); 7–22.

Rostovtzeff, M. I. *The Social and Economic History of the Hellenistic World.* Oxford, 1941.

Roth, Cecil. *A History of the Jews of England.* Oxford, 1964.

————. "Immanuel Aboab's Proselytization of the Marranos." *Jewish Quarterly Review* 23 (1932–33): 121–62.

————. "Leone da Modena and England." *Transactions of the Jewish Historical Society of England* 11 (1928): 206–27.

————. "New Notes on Pre-Emancipation Jewish Artists." *Hebrew Union College Annual* 17 (1942–43): 499–510.

Rowley, H. H. *Israel's Mission.* London, 1939.

————. *The Missionary Message of Israel.* London, 1945.

Rubenstein, Richard. "Intermarriage and Conversion." *Reconstructionist* 28 (April 20, 1962): 11–21.

Ruppin, Arthur. *The Jews in the Modern World.* London, 1934.

Samuel, Maurice. *Race, Nation and People in the Jewish Bible.* Syracuse, 1967.

Schechter, Solomon. "An Unknown Khazar Document." *Jewish Quarterly Review*, o.s. 3 (1912–13).

Schoeps, Hans-Joachim. "Philosemitism in the Baroque Period." *Jewish Quarterly Review* 47 (1956–57): 139–44.

Schürer, Emil. *A History of the Jewish People in the Time of Jesus Christ.* Edinburgh, 1905.

Sefer Hasidim. Berlin, 1924.

Shanks, Herschel. "Jewish-Gentile Intermarriage: Facts and Trends." *Commentary* 16 (1953): 370–75.

Sherwin-White, A. N. *Racial Prejudice in Imperial Rome.* Cambridge, 1967.

Silberman, Lou H. "Reprobation, Prohibition, Invalidity: An Examination of the Halachic Development Concerning Intermarriage." *CCAR Journal* 15 (1968): 2–15.

Silcox, Clarice E., and Fisher, Galen M. *Catholics, Jews and Protestants.* New York, 1934.

Simon, John Oswald. "Missionary Judaism." *Jewish Quarterly Review*, o.s. 5 (1893): 664–79.

————. "The Mission of Israel." *Fortnightly Review*, n.s. 60 (1896): 577–89.

————. "The Mission of Israel: A Reply." *Jewish Quarterly Review*, o.s. 9 (1897): 177–223, 403–28.

Singer, S. "Early Translations and Translators of the Jewish Liturgy in England." *Transactions of the Jewish Historical Society of England* 3 (1899): 36–71.

Sklare, Marshall. *America's Jews.* New York, 1971.

————, and Greenblum, Joseph. *Jewish Identity on the Suburban Frontier.* New York, 1967.

Stern, Henry A. *Wanderings Among the Falashas in Abyssinia.* London, 1862.

Ullendorff, Edward. *The Ethiopians.* 2nd ed. London, 1965.

Vetulani, Adam. "The Jews of Medieval Poland." *Jewish Journal of Sociology* 4 (1962): 274–94.

Wacholder, Ben Zion. "Attitudes Towards Proselytizing in the Classical Halakah." *Historia Judaica* 20 (1958): 77–96.

————. "Cases of Proselytizing in the Tosafist Responsa." *Jewish Quarterly Review* 51 (1960–61): 288–315.

————. "The Halakah and the Proselytizing of Slaves During the Gaonic Era." *Historia Judaica* 18 (1956): 89–106.

Watt, W. Montgomery. *Islam and the Integration of Society.* London, 1961.

Weber, Max. *Ancient Judaism.* Glencoe, Ill., 1952.

————. *General Economic History.* Glencoe, Ill., 1950.

Weisbrod, Robert G. "Israel and the Black Hebrew Israelites." *Judaism* 24 (Winter 1975): 23–38.

Wilde, Robert. *The Treatment of the Jews in the Greek Christian Writers of the First Three Centuries.* Washington, 1949.

Wischnitzer, Mark. *A History of Jewish Crafts and Guilds.* New York, 1965.

Wolfson, Harry A. *Philo.* Cambridge, Mass., 1948.

Wright, G. Ernest, ed. *The Bible and the Ancient Near East.* New York, 1961.

Zeitlin, Solomon. "Beginnings of Christianity and Judaism." *Jewish Quarterly Review* (1936–37): 385–98.

————. "The Jews, Race, Nation, or Religion—Which?" *Jewish Quarterly Review* (1935–36): 313-47.

————. "The Offspring of Intermarriage." *Jewish Quarterly Review* 51 (1960–61): 135–40.

————. "Proselytes and Proselytism During the Second Commonwealth and the Early Tannaitic Period." In *Harry Austryn Wolfson Jubilee Volume,* vol. 2, pp. 871–81. Jerusalem, 1965.

————. *The Rise and Fall of the Judean State.* Philadelphia, 1962.

————. "Who Is a Jew?" *Jewish Quarterly Review* 49 (1958–59): 241–70.

Index

Compiled by Robert J. Milch

169